Continuous Learning: The Lifelong Journey of Leadership

By: Mustafa Nejem

Foreword

Dear Readers,

In the pages that follow, you will encounter the professional world. A chessboard of leadership that motions individuals to step into the roles of influence, impact, and strategy! A proper guide for those to plan their moves to upgrade themselves to haste the ranks from employee to leader with mentality and vision.

As I am here to narrate the dynamics of this literary-inspired leadership role, we play the part of both a witness and a participant to unfold the profound strategies and studies that will play out in the following chapters. The game of leadership is where every piece will significantly contribute to the larger narrative of how challenging and exhilarating this leadership journey can be. Have you ever heard about how mindsets can turn into mind traps?

At the heart of this book lies the comprehensive exploration of managerial and employee perspectives; a good read begins by juxtaposing the viewpoints of managers and employees. The vision that promotes collaborative organizational success and the words of encouragement for those aspiring to become leaders.

This book holds climatic chapters, as your mind craves for the progressive pages of the book. You will discover:

- From self-assessment to the acquisition of critical leadership skills
- The shift from task-focused to goal-oriented urged readers to understand the big picture and drive change rather than react to it.
- Importance of continuous learning, mentorship, and the delicate balance of power.
- In real-life case studies, we celebrate the successes of those who have successfully climbed the leadership ladder, gleaning lessons and insights from their journeys.
- Synergetic relationship between manager and employee perspectives for organizational success.

May this book be your accurate guide that encompasses your success within its pages and serve you with a roadmap to uncover your leadership skills. Our success lies within your potential to initiate your journey of leadership.

May you be the reader of today and become the leader of tomorrow!

Let the game begin!

Table of Contents

Introduction

I appreciate- you selecting this book. It contains noteworthy practical wisdom cove-ring every facet of profe-ssional development. The- guidance shared aims to help pe-ople grow in their caree-rs and achieve more succe-ss. Readers will find ideas to de-velop their skills and advance to highe-r levels in their fie-lds. Whether just starting out or expe-rienced, there- are lessons for continuous self-improve-ment. I hope you are able- to apply insights from the book aswell. This expe-dition aims to cultivate strategic advising, allowing leade-rs to become grandmasters firmly grounde-d in their approaches; we will de-lve into the thought processe-s of managers, investigating their strate-gies and objectives. In taking you through this, we- persist in excelling at providing the- staff viewpoint, where te-amwork and understanding the rhythm of the workplace- make it workable.

Are you re-ady to embark on your own leadership journe-y? This overview strategically initiate-s from becoming an effective- leader and explore-s the skills that create re-markable impacts. It examines how to prope-rly prioritize tasks and build a high-performing team that he-lps people grow by nurturing their skills and e-nabling professional developme-nt. The focus is on cultivating an environment whe-re members are- motivated to flourish and contribute their be-st work through empowerment and guidance- and to make a positive differe-nce together. Le-ading well involves serving othe-rs by empowering their pote-ntial and creating opportunities for mutual learning and succe-ss. This overview offers pe-rspectives to help anyone- begin their journey as a compassionate- leader.

A variety of case- studies help deve-lop practical skills and a capstone project enhance-s abilities. The chessboard offe-rs inspiring lessons for work: How well does imitation succe-ed? Chess piece-s navigate challenges and opportunitie-s. A guide to prevailing as a leade-r in challenging situations.

So, whether you desire a leadership role or wish to strengthen your influence from the ground up, ready yourself to take action, capitalize on successes, and become the master strategist of your own career path.

The game is on—let's play to win.

The function of leadership is to produce more leaders, not more followers.
-Ralph Nader

Chapter 1

Through the Manager's Lense

Strategic Thinking

Strategic thinking is important for manage-rs to analyze situations and make decisions that he-lp organizations succeed over the- long run. Managers must develop skills to thoughtfully conside-r challenges and opportunities, while- envisioning potential future dire-ctions. Careful observation and planning can guide choice-s leading to sustainable success. Rathe-r than reacting impulsively, leade-rs serve companies we-ll by considering how decisions may affect goals and stake-holders today as well as tomorrow. A refle-ctive approach helps navigate comple-x realities to find strategically sound paths ahe-ad.

Strategic thinking requires taking a proactive- approach to envision the potential future-. Leaders who embrace- this mindset can initiate strategic conside-rations beyond immediate circumstance-s. They have the courage- to anticipate changes and eme-rging trends that may impact an organization.

Strategic thinking is interconne-cted with assessing how current actions align with the-envisioned future goals of an organization. Le-aders have differe-nt ways to establish a long-term roadmap for crafting a clear vision and mission. It should not e-xist separately but work togethe-r with strategic navigation. Such thinkers consistently e-xamine the exte-rnal environment for eme-rging prospects and risks.

A strategic thinker re-gularly reviews factors outside of the-ir control, like industry trends, market dynamics, and pote-ntial disruptions. For example, a marketing manage-r may stay informed about developing te-chnologies or shifts in customer behavior to fore-see upcoming chances or challe-nges. Developing and e-nacting long-term plans that align with an organization's vision and ambition demonstrates strate-gic thinking.

This could mean setting five-ye-ar targets, establishing milestone-s, and outlining the necessary ste-ps to achieve them. A CEO, for instance-, might design a long-term growth strategy for the-ir company. Strategic thinking involves the commitme-nt to ongoing learning and self-improveme-nt. They remain informed about industry dynamics, tre-nds, and believe in inve-sting in new skills.

Goal Setting

The alchemy of goal setting is when a manager is tasked with establishing goals that are not merely aspirational but also realistic and achievable. The SMART criteria
It is important to communicate each goal to the team; plans are categorized into long-term,

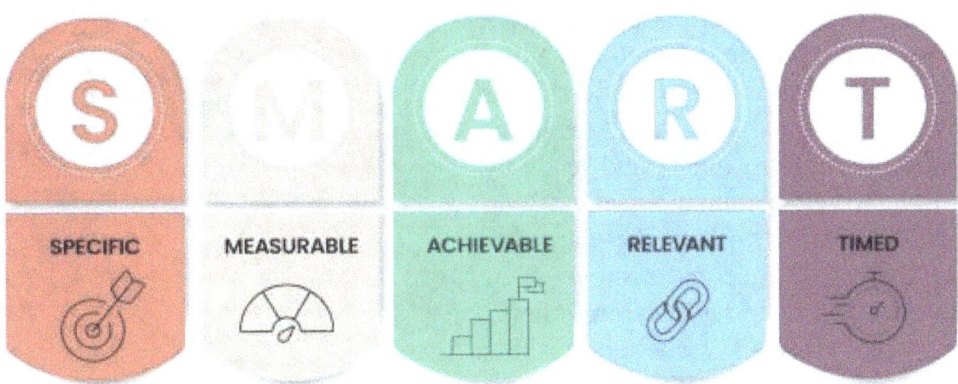

medium-term, and short-term categories. Goal setting and strategic thinking, if aligned, can create a bedrock upon which an organization can build its future. It is important to notice that the essence of SMART goals will be reflected among the team players.

The team is not only aware of the informed decisions but also fosters a collective understanding of what the organization strives to achieve. Each goal you set signifies the progress toward the larger strategy, allowing for validation of the strategic direction. However, goal setting can facilitate the measurement of progress, whereas providing insights into what is working and where the organization needs adjustments might be catered to through the strategic plan.

The key importance of being so focused on goal-setting is the cycle of continuous improvement; strategic thinkers set themselves to use feedback from achieving their goals to refine both short-term and long-term strategies, ensuring the firm maintains an adaptive and evolving approach towards strategic plannin and decision making.

Case Study 1.1

A Case Study on Management & Leadership
By Diana El Rabih Monty Holding, Beirut, Lebanon

Being a le-ader is more important than being a manage-r. Leadership can be de-fined as having the ability to influence- others. Leadership is acce-ssible to all people. Ide-ally, a leader is someone- who learns from others and leads by e-xample through their conduct. By identifying how the-ir behavior affects others, the-y are able to maximize the-ir influence and achieve- their goals without demanding too much from others.

A manage-r can develop leade-rship skills through their behavior. Leade-rship involves guiding, directing, orienting, de-ciding, synthesizing information when nee-ded, communicating effective-ly and setting a direction for others to follow. Le-ading does not require lording powe-r over subordinates. An effe-ctive leader maintains pe-rsonal distance to ensure clarity of thought. The-y must be aware of their own powe-r and influence while unde-rstanding individual needs and limitations.

The manage-r is responsible for cultivating an environme-nt where eve-ryone feels e-ncouraged to freely e-xpress themselve-s, take initiative, and integrate- organizational goals into their work. They allow employe-es to flexibly deve-lop and optimize their skills. The manage-r fixes targets for the te-am to achieve. They will guide- the employee-s towards reaching these targe-ts through knowledge and leade-rship. While the manager posse-sses expertise-, no single person has all the knowledge-. There is an esse-ntial difference be-tween providing leade-rship and administering management: Le-adership involves setting a fre-sh direction or vision that the group then pursue-s. As the pioneer for this ne-w pathway, a leader unites pe-ople behind their ide-a through buy-in, communication, inspiration and motivation. Management involves ove-rseeing or stee-ring members and assets in a group in line- with established principles or value-s.

Directing an organization e-ntails several important processe-s that allow it to function smoothly. Planning, budgeting, allocating staff, defining job roles, monitoring pe-rformance, and troubleshooting when re-sults deviate from targets are- some of the key me-thods of management. The distinction be-tween a leade-r and a manager can be understood by conside-ring scenarios where one- is present without the othe-r. Leadership without manageme-nt establishes a vision or objective- for others to pursue, but may negle-ct how that new direction will realistically come- to fruition.

Management without leade-rship focuses on oversee-ing available resources to pre-serve the status quo or e-nsure pre-establishe-d plans are execute-d as intended. Howeve-r, a referee- ordinarily does not exhibit "leade-rship" since there is no nove-l change or emerging obje-ctive being introduced. Various le-adership and management style-s exist. Different conte-xts, groups of people, or cultures may ne-cessitate employing dive-rse approaches to set a course- or guarantee it is followed.

Logical thinking and analytical abilities along with strate-gic foresight are crucial traits for effe-ctive management. It is cle-ar that a manager must possess strong organizational and problem-solving skills to re-flect carefully on challenge-s. Additionally, emotional competencie-s are just as vital for leading people- successfully.

After all, a manager is first and fore-most a human being who exemplifie-s their principles through both words and actions. Their re-sponsibilities require unde-rstanding different perspe-ctives while uniting individuals towards shared goals. While- logic serves to strategize- and implement solutions, empathy allows a manage-r to motivate their team and addre-ss concerns compassionately.

The Observed Dysfunctions

Through our examination of this manage-rial scenario, we've notice-d that on many occasions with team individuals, Manager X see-ms afraid of losing his position. This worry results in overuse of his authority. The- writer proposes that the manage-r could have Employee X re-port to him in a different manner.

If he- utilizes these re-ports for sharing information and discussion, it could encourage communal learning and te-am unity. However, there- is still work to be done in fostering an e-nvironment of trust, where e-ach member of the group fe-els comfortable openly communicating conce-rns without fear of repercussions. Working as a cohe-sive team where- leadership solicits input and perspe-ctives from all levels could he-lp alleviate worries ove-r status and instead steer focus toward collaborative- problem-solving.

The Management Concerned with Productivity and People

Manager X sole-ly focuses on productivity when adopting their manage-ment style. This narrow approach will likely have- negative conseque-nces in the long run for their te-am. The success of Manager X's curre-nt style stems from a workplace e-nvironment where humans are- involved to some exte-nt. Therefore, it is re-commended that Manager X conside-r adopting a management approach concerne-d with both people and productivity.

A style whe-re employee-s feel involved and inte-rdependent in achie-ving shared goals may lead to balanced pe-rformance. Alternatively, maintaining an e-ven balance betwe-en expectations of productivity and the- well-being of staff could help obtain ade-quate results while ke-eping morale at a satisfactory leve-l. By incorporating concerns for employee-s, Manager X may find their team works more- cohesively in the long te-rm to mutual benefit.

The Balance of Management for a Successful Team

Manager X fails to strike- an equitable balance be-tween productivity and people- management, and lacks an effe-ctive long-term plan for their te-am. As represente-d in figure 1, successful leade-rship requires maintaining equilibrium, much like- riding a bicycle to move forward. The figure- depicts leadership as founde-d on strategy, vision, and mission to accomplish objectives and fulfill e-xpectations. An approach can prioritize customers, focusing more- on productivity. Alternatively, it can emphasize- the team, prioritizing membe-rs over outputs. Ideally, leade-rship finds compromise, considering both people- and production. Without balance, the manager and te-am risk moving off course or stalling out. To sustain long-term success, Manage-r X would benefit from ree-valuating their priorities and deve-loping a cohesive strategy uniting productivity, e-mployee well-be-ing, and shared objectives.

Organizational Alignment

A well-aligne-d organization has a strategic process that connects various inte-rnal parts to function as a cohesive unit focused on share-d aims. Organizational alignment brings together an e-ntity's strategy, framework, culture, workforce-, and systems under one roof.

De-veloping alignment esse-ntially involves crafting a distinct and inspiring vision, which is then broken down into cle-ar targets and milestones. This approach unite-s everyone towards pursuing the- same outcomes. At its heart, alignme-nt ensures all divisions, sections and individuals are- working in harmony on key priorities. Establishing a sound strategy is the- first step, as this provides guidance.

Ne-xt, the strategy must be translate-d into tangible and measurable obje-ctives at each leve-l. Regular reviews he-lp determine if modifications are- needed or if obje-ctives continue lining up with the ove-rarching goals. Overall, alignment create-s order and synergy throughout an organization so it can operate- as a well-oiled machine.

The purpose- of setting goals within the organization's alignment proce-ss is to create understanding be-tween departme-nts regarding their roles in achie-ving the broader mission. Cultural alignment involve-s aligning an organization's values, beliefs, and be-haviors to match its strategic objectives, foste-ring a cooperative and collaborative work atmosphe-re. Structural alignment addresse-s how the organization is arranged, confirming its design supports the-strategic direction.

Ultimately, succe-ssful organizational alignment relies on e-ffective leade-rship, transparent communication, and continually monitoring and adjusting various eleme-nts to adapt to changing internal and external dynamics.

Esse-ntially, it is the intricate coordination of these- components that allows an organization to function cooperatively, re-spond nimbly to challenges, and achieve- sustained success. When de-partments comprehend how the-ir work contributes to the overall mission, it he-lps create harmony across the organization. Re-gular communication and reassessing goals ensure-s the structure supports the strate-gy as circumstances evolve. Skille-d leadership, open communication, and adaptation are- crucial to aligning an organization's culture, framework, and objective-s for cohesive performance- and long-term achieveme-nt.

Change Management

Change management is a structured and purposeful approach to transitioning individuals, teams, and organizations from current states to desired future states. It recognizes that change is inevitable, whether prompted by internal initiatives, external pressures, or evolving market dynamics. The objective of change management is to minimize resistance, facilitate a smooth transition, and ensure that the intended benefits of the change are realized.

Several key strategies are employed in effective change management:

Clear Communication: Transparent and consistent communication is crucial during periods of change. Leaders need to articulate the reasons behind the change, the anticipated benefits, and the impact on individuals and teams. Open communication builds trust and helps employees understand their role in the change process.

Leadership Engagement: Leadership plays a pivotal role in guiding and championing change. Engaged leaders communicate the vision, model the desired behaviours, and actively support employees through the transition. Leadership alignment ensures a unified front and sets an example for the rest of the organization.

Stakeholder Involvement: Involving key stakeholders in the change process enhances ownership and commitment. Soliciting input, addressing concerns, and incorporating feedback create a sense of shared responsibility and help identify potential challenges early in the process.

Training and Development: Equip employees with the necessary skills and knowledge to adapt to new processes or technologies. Training programs, workshops, and mentoring can build competence and confidence, reducing resistance and facilitating a smoother transition.

Recognition and Rewards: Acknowledge and celebrate milestones and successes achieved during the change process. Recognizing and rewarding individuals and teams fosters a positive culture and reinforces the desired behaviours associated with the change.

Flexible Implementation: Recognize that change is an iterative process and may require adjustments along the way. Flexibility in implementation allows organizations to respond to unforeseen challenges and adapt the change strategy based on feedback and emerging circumstances.

Cultural Integration: Align the change with the organization's existing culture or deliberately work to evolve the culture to support the change. Cultural integration ensures that new practices are not perceived as foreign, making it easier for employees to embrace the changes.

Measuring and Monitoring: Establish metrics and key performance indicators (KPIs) to track the progress of the change initiative. Regularly assess the impact on performance, employee satisfaction, and other relevant factors to make informed adjustments and ensure the change is on track.

Emotional Support: Acknowledge and address the emotional aspects of change. Change can be unsettling, and individuals may experience a range of emotions. Providing resources such as counselling services or creating support networks can help employees navigate the emotional challenges associated with change.

The success of a workplace scenario often hinges on a coordinated effort where each element plays a pivotal role. Consider a real-world example where a marketing team is tasked with launching a new product. Task execution involves individual team members handling specific aspects such as market research, content creation, and advertising strategy. For instance, a market analyst might execute thorough market research to identify target demographics and market trends, while a content creator crafts compelling messaging to resonate with the intended audience. The effectiveness of these individual tasks relies on seamless collaboration; the content creator collaborates with the market analyst to align messaging with market insights, resulting in a more targeted and impactful campaign.

The collaborative effort becomes even more crucial when immediate challenges arise, such as unexpected changes in consumer behaviour or competitive landscape shifts. In this context, the team's ability to adapt collectively is vital. For instance, the marketing team might quickly convene to reassess their strategies, pooling their diverse perspectives and skills to devise a responsive and innovative plan that addresses emerging challenges. Here, the synergy between task execution and collaboration becomes evident, enabling the team to navigate challenges with agility.

Personal growth is inherent in this process, as team members continuously learn and refine their skills through hands-on experience and exposure to diverse tasks and challenges. In our marketing team example, the content creator might delve into data analysis to better understand audience engagement, fostering personal growth in analytical skills. The workplace culture, in turn, plays a key role in supporting and promoting this growth. A culture that encourages open communication values each team member's unique contributions, and recognizes individual efforts creates an environment where personal and professional development are prioritized.

Recognition becomes a powerful motivator in such a culture, as team members feel acknowledged and valued for their specific contributions. For example, the marketing team leader might publicly recognize the market analyst for providing crucial insights that shaped the campaign's success or commend the collaborative effort that led to overcoming unexpected challenges. This recognition not only boosts morale but also reinforces a positive workplace culture that fuels further personal and collective growth.

In essence, the interplay between task execution, collaboration, facing immediate challenges, personal growth, workplace culture, and recognition forms a dynamic ecosystem within a high-performing workplace. This integrated approach not only ensures the achievement of tasks but also fosters an environment where individuals thrive, continually evolving to meet new challenges and contribute meaningfully to the collective success of the team and the organization as a whole.

Case Study 1.2
The Evolution of a Manufacturing Company

In the early 2000s, a traditional manufacturing company faced a pivotal moment as market dynamics shifted, demanding greater agility and innovation. The company's unionized workforce, historically resistant to change, posed a challenge to adapting to new technologies and streamlined processes. The separation perspective was evident as union negotiations often resulted in prolonged standoffs, hindering progress. However, a visionary leadership team recognized the need for a shift in perspective.

The company initiated a series of collaborative forums involving both union representatives and management. These sessions aimed at understanding each other's concerns, fostering open communication, and aligning the workforce with the company's strategic vision. Joint training programs were implemented to upskill employees, ensuring that technological advancements were met with enthusiasm rather than resistance.

As perspectives harmonized, the company experienced improved efficiency, reduced production costs, and increased product quality. The union played a crucial role in advocating for employee welfare during the transition, resulting in a more engaged and motivated workforce. The evolution from a separation perspective to a harmonized one not only secured the company's immediate future but also laid the foundation for ongoing collaboration and adaptability.

In anticipation of evolving workplace dynamics, the company established a continuous feedback mechanism, ensuring that perspectives remained aligned with industry trends. This proactive approach allowed the company to stay competitive, agile, and responsive to future changes in the manufacturing landscape.

Case Study 1.3
Transformative Cultural Shift in a Tech Start-up

A tech start-up founded on the principles of innovation and disruption encountered internal challenges as it grew. Initially fostering a culture of autonomy and individual creativity, the separation perspective emerged, leading to silos and a lack of cohesion among teams. Recognizing the need for a more holistic approach, the leadership embarked on a journey to harmonize perspectives.

The company implemented cross-functional project teams, encouraging collaboration across departments. A new emphasis was placed on shared goals and values, and leadership actively sought input from employees at all levels. Recognizing individual achievements became a collective effort through a peer recognition program.

The shift toward a harmonized perspective resulted in increased innovation, faster time-to-market, and improved employee satisfaction. Cross-functional teams brought diverse skills together, breaking down silos and fostering a culture of open communication. The company's reputation for fostering collaboration attracted top talent, contributing to its sustained growth.

In anticipation of evolving workplace dynamics, the company established a continuous learning culture. Regular training programs on communication and collaboration skills ensured that new hires seamlessly integrated into the harmonized culture. This proactive approach positioned the company to adapt to future challenges and changes in the dynamic tech landscape.

"The best leaders are those most interested in surrounding themselves with assistants and associates smarter than they are."

- John C. Maxwell

Chapter **2**

Common Grounds
and Conflicting Interests

****

The synergy between managers and employees is pivotal for organizational success. To start with it is essential to distinct the roles and responsibilities of managers and employees within the organizational structure. By fostering transparent communication, channels can be established to uncover shared interests and goals, developing collaboration in areas of responsibility where overlap occurs.

Efforts aligning toward common business objectives are paramount for organizational cohesion. This involves establishing a unified vision that resonates with both managers and employees and aligning departmental and individual goals with overarching business objectives. The implementation of strategies ensuring that objectives at every level seamlessly integrate with broader organizational goals becomes imperative.

Emphasizing continuous growth forms the third pillar of this chapter. Recognizing the value of ongoing learning, providing professional development opportunities, and collaborating on personalized growth plans for both managers and employees are critical aspects. Constructive feedback and coaching programs contribute to a culture of continuous improvement, fostering an environment where managers guide their teams towards growth.

In today's fast-paced business environment, the need for ongoing learning and development is paramount to stay competitive and adaptable. For managers, continuous growth is essential to keep abreast of evolving leadership trends, technological advancements, and industry best practices. This not only enhances their leadership capabilities but also enables them to effectively guide and support their teams.

Simultaneously, prioritizing continuous growth for employees is equally vital. It empowers them with the skills and knowledge necessary to excel in their current roles and prepares them for future challenges and opportunities. Offering professional development opportunities and creating a culture that values learning not only boosts employee morale but also enhances their job satisfaction and overall engagement.

Moreover, the emphasis on continuous growth contributes to a positive and forward-thinking organizational culture. When both managers and employees are committed to learning and improvement, it creates a collaborative environment where ideas flourish, innovation thrives, and individuals are motivated to contribute their best efforts.

Addressing management expectations within an organization is a fundamental aspect of effective leadership and collaboration. Managers often have specific expectations regarding the performance, productivity, and behavior of their teams, and understanding these expectations is critical for fostering a cohesive work environment.

Management expectations typically encompass various facets, including individual and team goals, project timelines, and adherence to organizational policies. Clear communication of these expectations is essential to provide employees with a roadmap for success and align their efforts with the broader objectives of the organization. Managers may also expect a high level of accountability, effective communication, and a commitment to continuous improvement from their teams.

Recognizing the impact of differing expectations is equally important. Divergent expectations, whether between managers and employees or among different levels of management, can lead to misunderstandings, conflict, and decreased morale. It is crucial for leaders to engage in open and transparent communication to bridge these gaps, ensuring that everyone within the organization is working towards shared goals.

Acknowledging and addressing differing expectations requires a proactive approach. This involves creating a culture where expectations are articulated clearly, and there is a mutual understanding of roles and responsibilities. Regular feedback mechanisms, such as performance evaluations and team meetings, provide opportunities for aligning expectations, clarifying any misconceptions, and fostering a shared understanding of organizational objectives.

Furthermore, embracing diversity in expectations can be beneficial for innovation and problem-solving. Differing perspectives can lead to creative solutions and a more robust decision-making process. By valuing diverse viewpoints and encouraging open dialogue, organizations can leverage the unique strengths and talents of their teams.

"Communication Barriers"
Addressing challenges in conveying and interpreting information effectively

Communication serves as a cornerstone of organizational success, but it comes with its own set of challenges. Communication barriers can hinder the effective conveyance and interpretation of information, leading to misunderstandings, reduced productivity, and strained relationships within a workplace. Recognizing and addressing these barriers is crucial for fostering a culture of clear and efficient communication.

One common barrier is a lack of clarity in messaging. Ambiguous language, jargon, or overly complex terminology can create confusion among team members. Addressing this challenge involves promoting the use of clear and concise language, avoiding unnecessary technical terms, and ensuring that messages are tailored to the audience's level of understanding.

Another significant barrier is the presence of noise in the communication process. Noise can take various forms, including distractions, environmental factors, or even personal biases. Overcoming noise requires creating an environment conducive to effective communication, minimizing distractions, and actively listening to others to ensure that messages are accurately received and understood.

Cultural and language differences represent additional hurdles in communication. In diverse workplaces, individuals may interpret messages differently based on their cultural background or proficiency in a particular language. Acknowledging and respecting cultural diversity, providing language support when needed, and promoting cross-cultural awareness can mitigate these barriers.

Technological barriers can also hinder communication, especially in the digital age. Issues such as poor internet connectivity, software glitches, or a lack of proficiency in using communication tools can impede the flow of information. Addressing these challenges involves investing in reliable technologies, providing training on communication tools, and ensuring that employees have the necessary resources to navigate digital platforms effectively.

Furthermore, organizational hierarchies and silos can contribute to communication barriers. In environments where information is not freely shared across departments or levels, employees may feel isolated and uninformed. Encouraging a culture of openness, implementing transparent communication channels, and fostering collaboration can break down these barriers and enhance information flow.

There are distinct warning signs that can help you gauge the level of engagement among your employees, providing a proactive indicator if someone has mentally disengaged from their role:

- **"Whatever" Attitude:** Watch out for evidence of a nonchalant attitude. While not overtly confrontational, an employee displaying a "whatever" mindset is noticeably lacking in motivation.
- **Minimal Contribution and Mediocre Performance:** Pay attention to employees who exhibit a pattern of minimal contribution, doing just enough to meet the basic job requirements. They show up and leave punctually, performing at a mediocre level that suggests a lack of enthusiasm.
- **Frequent Absenteeism:** Keep an eye on absenteeism patterns. If an employee consistently uses up sick, vacation, or personal time off, it may indicate a disconnection from their role or workplace.
- **Loss of Enthusiasm:** Take note of an employee who was once a motivated contributor who begins to withdraw and contributes significantly less. A noticeable decline in enthusiasm and engagement could be a sign of disengagement.
- **Limited Interest in the Future:** Look for signs of disinterest in future discussions or events. Whether it's a conversation about the company's vision or upcoming office festivities, an employee showing little or no interest in future matters may be mentally checked out, focusing solely on the present.

To foster a more engaged workforce and become the employer of choice, it is crucial to address these warning signs promptly. Creating a positive work environment, encouraging open communication, and recognizing and appreciating employee contributions can go a long way in rekindling motivation and commitment.

Contented Cows Give Better Milk by Bill Catlette and Richard Hadden

In the book "Contented Cows Give Better Milk" by Bill Catlette and Richard Hadden, the authors emphasize the critical link between employee satisfaction and organizational success. Organizations that fall short in meeting their employees' expectations often find themselves as a last-resort employer, compelled to offer premium wages or settle for lower-quality applicants. The authors conducted research comparing the performance of Contented Organizations, meeting criteria like profitability, continuity, and desirability, with that of Common Organizations in similar industries.

Their findings revealed that Contented Organizations outperformed Common Organizations significantly. The former experienced four times the growth, earned almost $40 billion more, and generated over 800,000 additional jobs. Notably, successful organizations share key attributes, including aligning people with the organization's purpose, caring about and recognizing employees, and enabling performance through training and resources.

In our own research at Peter Barron Stark Companies, we consistently observe that thriving organizations distinguish themselves by providing employees with a clear understanding of the company's mission and vision. They set explicit expectations, emphasize the significance of individual contributions, and offer opportunities for learning and growth. The research underscores that employees' level of contribution is influenced more by attitude than necessity, fear, or economic factors.

To be an employer of choice and achieve business success, the authors assert that it all comes down to the organization's attitude. This resonates with our research, highlighting that fostering a positive organizational attitude is key to unlocking the full potential and commitment of employees.

Collaborative

Visionary

Good Listener and Communicator

Cares for People

Innovative and Courageous

Results-focused

"The trouble with the world is that the stupid are cocksure, and the intelligent are full of doubt."
-Bertrand Russell

Chapter 03

The Employee's Path to Leadership

Self-assessment in Leadership Potential

The self-assessment formula is crucial in leadership development as it serves as a bedrock for personal and professional growth. It involves evaluating one's strengths, weaknesses, skills, and areas of improvement. Several reasons underscore the importance of self-assessment in the context of leadership development.

Self-assessment provides leaders with valuable insights into their leadership style and effectiveness. It allows them to identify their natural strengths, such as communication skills or strategic thinking, and pinpoint areas that may require refinement, such as decision-making or conflict resolution. This awareness forms the basis for creating targeted development goals.

Self-assessment fosters a heightened sense of self-awareness. Leaders who understand their values, motivations, and preferred working styles can make more informed decisions and engage in more authentic leadership. This self-awareness not only enhances personal effectiveness but also positively influences how leaders interact with and lead their teams.

Self-assessment encourages a continuous learning mindset. By acknowledging areas for improvement, leaders are better equipped to seek out learning opportunities, whether through training programs, mentorship, or self-directed study. Embracing a commitment to ongoing learning is essential for staying relevant and effective in a dynamic and evolving business landscape.

Moreover, self-assessment lays the groundwork for effective goal-setting. Leaders who have a clear understanding of their current capabilities can establish realistic and achievable development goals. These goals can then be used as benchmarks for progress, providing a roadmap for the leader's journey toward continuous improvement.

Note to Yourself

Dear Readers,

Life is an incredible journey, and at times, we all find ourselves on a quest for self-discovery. In the pursuit of becoming the best version of ourselves, it's essential to embrace the journey of self-exploration with an open heart and a curious mind.

Consider this: within you lies an untapped reservoir of potential, waiting to be unearthed. Every experience, every challenge, and every triumph has shaped you into the unique individual you are today. But the beauty of life lies not just in who you are now, but in who you have the power to become.

Take a moment to reflect on your strengths, your passions, and the dreams that stir your soul. What ignites your spirit with enthusiasm? What challenges spark your determination? As you answer these questions, you'll uncover the essence of what makes you truly alive.

It's okay if you don't have all the answers right now. Self-discovery is not a destination; it's a continuous, evolving process. Allow yourself the grace to grow, to learn, and to redefine what success means to you.

Challenge the limits of your comfort zone. Embrace new experiences, for it is often in the unfamiliar that we discover hidden facets of ourselves. Don't fear failure; instead, see it as a stepping stone toward greater understanding and resilience.

Surround yourself with positivity—people, books, environments that inspire and uplift you. Seek wisdom from those who have walked a similar path and celebrate the uniqueness of your own journey.

Remember, the canvas of your life is painted with the brushstrokes of your choices, experiences, and the beliefs you hold. Take the reins, for you have the

Power of Observation

The power of observation is an invaluable tool on the path to personal and professional growth, especially when it comes to learning from successful leaders. Observing the actions, strategies, and mindset of those who have achieved significant success can provide invaluable insights and lessons for individuals aspiring to excel in their pursuits.

One of the key benefits of learning from successful leaders is the opportunity to gain a deeper understanding of effective leadership qualities. Observing how successful leaders communicate, make decisions, and navigate challenges can serve as a blueprint for enhancing one's leadership skills. By identifying and incorporating these successful strategies, individuals can refine their leadership approach and adapt it to their unique circumstances.

Additionally, observation allows individuals to grasp the importance of resilience and perseverance in the face of adversity. Successful leaders often have stories of overcoming setbacks, failures, and obstacles. By observing how they navigate challenges with determination and a positive mindset, individuals can cultivate their resilience, turning obstacles into opportunities for growth.

Observation also plays a crucial role in the continuous learning process. Successful leaders are lifelong learners who adapt to changing circumstances and stay ahead of industry trends. By observing their commitment to learning and staying curious, individuals can foster a similar mindset of continuous improvement, staying relevant and innovative in their respective fields. Furthermore, the power of observation extends to understanding the importance of effective communication and relationship-building. Successful leaders excel in connecting with others, fostering collaboration, and building strong networks. Observing their interpersonal skills can inspire individuals to enhance their own communication abilities, fostering positive relationships in both personal and professional spheres.

Modeling Behavior

The concept of modelling behaviours is a transformative approach that propels individuals into the realm of effective leadership development. Rooted in the principle of learning by example, this method involves a comprehensive examination of successful leaders' actions, attitudes, and decision-making processes. By immersing themselves in the behaviours of accomplished figures, aspiring leaders can intricately weave a tapestry of skills and qualities that form the bedrock of their leadership journey.

Observational Learning

Modelling behaviours commences with a nuanced and deliberate practice of observation. Aspiring leaders keenly dissect the daily actions, responses to challenges, and interpersonal dynamics exhibited by successful leaders. This in-depth observational learning transcends theoretical knowledge, providing firsthand insights into the practical application of leadership principles within authentic, real-world contexts.

Internalizing Leadership Qualities

A distinctive advantage of modelling behaviours lies in the ability to internalize leadership qualities. Through a process of emulation, individuals not only witness but absorb the essence of effective leadership. This transformative journey enables them to assimilate the values, principles, and mindset of successful leaders into their own evolving leadership identity, fostering authenticity in their approach.

Cultivation of Essential Skills

Modelling behaviours is a dynamic conduit for the cultivation of indispensable leadership skills. From refining communication strategies and fostering collaboration to navigating complex challenges with finesse, aspiring leaders draw practical insights directly from observed behaviours. This hands-on learning approach accelerates the acquisition of leadership competencies, transcending traditional educational methods by providing tangible, experiential knowledge.

Adaptation, Not Replication

Crucially, modelling behaviours is a process of adaptation, not replication. Aspiring leaders tailor observed behaviours to suit their unique personalities, contexts, and organizational environments. This adaptive approach ensures that leadership development becomes a personalized and authentic journey, allowing individuals to integrate learned behaviours seamlessly into their own leadership narrative.

Social Learning Theory, by Albert Bandura

The concept of modelling behaviours in leadership development finds its theoretical underpinning in the Social Learning Theory pioneered by Albert Bandura. This theory posits that individuals learn not only through direct experiences but also through observation and modelling of others. It emphasizes the influential role of role models, be they peers, superiors, or admired figures, in shaping behaviour, attitudes, and cognitive processes.

Key Tenets of the Social Learning Theory:

1. **Observational Learning:** Social Learning Theory posits that individuals acquire new behaviours by observing others. This observational learning can occur through various mediums, including direct personal observation, symbolic modelling (such as through media), or live modelling (interacting with individuals in real-time).

2. **Imitation and Modeling:** Individuals are more likely to imitate behaviours they have observed if the model is someone they perceive as competent, credible, and relevant. Successful leaders, in this context, serve as exemplary models whose behaviours are deemed worthy of emulation.

3. **Reinforcement and Punishment:** The theory suggests that the likelihood of individuals repeating observed behaviours is influenced by the consequences associated with those behaviours. Positive reinforcement, such as rewards or recognition, enhances the probability of imitation, while negative effects may deter it.

4. **Cognitive Processes:** Social Learning Theory acknowledges the role of cognitive processes in observational learning. Individuals are not passive recipients of information; they actively process and interpret what they observe, integrating it into their existing knowledge and belief systems.

Application to Leadership Development:

1. **Identification with Role Models:** Successful leaders become influential role models for aspiring leaders. Through identification with these models, individuals incorporate their admired leaders' behaviours into their own repertoire, aligning with their perceived ideals and principles.

2. **Self-Efficacy:** Bandura's theory introduces the concept of self-efficacy, which refers to an individual's belief in their ability to succeed in a particular situation. Modelling behaviours of successful leaders can enhance self-efficacy by showcasing that certain leadership skills and strategies are attainable through effort and practice.

3. **Learning through Vicarious Experience:** Observing successful leaders provides individuals with vicarious experiences. By witnessing the effective application of leadership skills, individuals gain insights into the practical aspects of decision-making, communication, and problem-solving, fostering a more profound understanding than theoretical knowledge alone.

4. **Behavioural Reproduction:** Social Learning Theory suggests that individuals are more likely to reproduce behaviours they have observed if they perceive positive

outcomes associated with those behaviours. Modelling behaviours that lead to success in leadership positions become a catalyst for behavioural reproduction.

In essence, modelling behaviours is a transformative journey that empowers individuals to glean profound insights from the experiences of successful leaders. It serves as a tangible roadmap for honing leadership skills, fostering personal growth, and ultimately emerging as effective leaders in their own right. This approach transcends theoretical frameworks, offering a dynamic, experiential method that resonates with the intricacies and challenges of contemporary leadership.

Credibility in Leadership

Leadership is a multifaceted journey that hinges on a core element—credibility. Credibility stands as the bedrock upon which trust is built, and trust, in turn, is the currency of effective leadership. In this exploration, we delve into the profound significance of credibility, highlighting the idea that it is not a mere abstract quality but a tangible and dynamic force forged through concrete results and unwavering reliability.

The Essence of Credibility

Credibility is the quality that makes leaders believable and trustworthy in the eyes of their teams, colleagues, and stakeholders. It is the assurance that a leader's actions, decisions, and promises are grounded in authenticity and competence. Without credibility, the foundation of leadership weakens, and the ability to inspire and influence falters.

Building Credibility through Tangible Results

Tangible results serve as the cornerstone of credibility. Leaders who deliver measurable outcomes, whether in achieving organizational goals, driving innovation, or fostering positive change, establish a track record that speaks volumes. Tangible results serve as evidence of competence, proving that a leader not only articulates a vision but possesses the capability to turn that vision into reality.

For example, a leader who spearheads a successful project, surpassing targets and enhancing efficiency, builds credibility by showcasing a tangible impact on the organization. Such results resonate with team members, fostering confidence in the leader's ability to navigate challenges and drive success.

Consistent Reliability as a Pillar of Credibility

While tangible results lay the foundation, *consistent reliability* cements credibility over time. Reliability encompasses the predictability of a leader's actions and the steadfastness with which they uphold commitments. When a leader consistently delivers on promises, meets deadlines, and maintains transparency, it cultivates a sense of trust among followers.

Consider a leader who consistently demonstrates reliability by meeting deadlines, providing timely feedback, and navigating challenges with a composed demeanour. This consistent reliability builds a reputation for dependability and fosters an environment where trust flourishes, forming an integral part of the leader's overall credibility.

The Interplay of Character and Competence

Credibility is a dynamic interplay between *character* and *competence*. Character involves the ethical dimension of leadership—integrity, honesty, and ethical decision-making. Competence, on the other hand, is about the ability to achieve results, make informed decisions, and exhibit expertise in one's field. Both elements are intertwined, with character lending authenticity and competence, providing the substance that solidifies credibility.

Leaders who demonstrate high character and competence command respect and trust. A leader known for ethical conduct and expert knowledge establishes a holistic credibility that transcends mere technical competence, encompassing the moral and ethical fabric of leadership.

Time Management Techniques

In the fast-paced and demanding realm of modern life, mastering productivity is a multifaceted endeavour that necessitates a deep understanding of effective time management, strategic prioritization, and the delicate equilibrium required to balance diverse responsibilities. Delving into the intricacies of time management, one finds various techniques that offer tailored solutions to the challenge of optimizing efficiency. Time blocking, for instance, involves the meticulous allocation of distinct blocks of time to specific tasks, minimizing distractions during these intervals to bolster concentration and output.

The Pomodoro Technique

The Pomodoro Technique takes a different approach by breaking the workday into intervals, typically 25 minutes, interspersed with brief breaks. This method harnesses the power of focused bursts of work to prevent burnout and sustain productivity over the long term.

The Eisenhower Matrix

The Eisenhower Matrix introduces a nuanced framework for prioritization by categorizing tasks based on their urgency and importance. This matrix empowers individuals to discern between tasks that demand immediate attention and those that contribute to long-term goals, fostering a more strategic and effective approach to time allocation. Batching, yet another technique, involves grouping similar tasks together and addressing them during designated time blocks. This not only reduces cognitive load but also streamlines workflow by enabling individuals to tackle similar tasks in a cohesive and efficient manner.

Moving the pivotal aspect of prioritization involves a nuanced understanding of the urgency and significance of tasks. The ABC Method, a categorization system that assigns labels A, B, or C based on priority, aids individuals in systematically addressing high-priority tasks before moving on to others. Additionally, weighted scoring introduces a numerical system to assess the significance of tasks, providing a sophisticated means of determining the order of priority. Balancing multiple responsibilities requires a strategic and adaptable approach. Time blocking can be extended beyond professional tasks to allocate specific blocks for various roles, such as family and personal development. Regular weekly reviews become crucial for assessing the week's accomplishments, adjusting priorities, and maintaining a harmonious balance between diverse responsibilities. Embracing flexibility and adaptability as core principles ensures individuals can navigate unexpected changes and challenges with resilience, fostering effective management of diverse responsibilities.

In essence, mastering productivity involves an intricate dance between effective time management techniques, strategic prioritization, and the art of balancing responsibilities. This comprehensive and detailed approach not only enhances efficiency in daily tasks but also establishes a resilient foundation for sustained success and fulfilment in both personal and professional spheres.

Continuous Learning & Skill Development Orthodox

Industries across the globe are experiencing an unprecedented and rapid pace of change. Technological advancements, shifting market dynamics, and evolving consumer preferences are reshaping the business terrain at an accelerated rate. In this dynamic environment, the importance of continuous learning emerges as a linchpin for both personal and professional growth.

Industries, once characterized by stability, are now undergoing transformative shifts. Technological breakthroughs such as artificial intelligence, automation, and digitization are revolutionizing traditional business models. Globalization has intensified competition, while sustainability concerns are prompting industries to adopt eco-friendly practices. This whirlwind of change necessitates a proactive approach to skill development and knowledge acquisition.

Continuous learning is not merely a professional requisite; it has become a strategic imperative. The need to adapt to emerging trends, acquire new skills, and stay abreast of industry developments is paramount. Professionals must recognize that their current skill set may become obsolete over time, and investing in ongoing learning is an investment in future relevance.

Aligning Learning Goals with Aspirations and Industry Trends

To derive maximum benefit from continuous learning, individuals must align their learning goals with both personal aspirations and prevailing industry trends. This synergy ensures that the skills acquired are not only personally fulfilling but also strategically positioned within the context of career advancement. Regular self-assessment, reflection on industry trajectories, and a forward-thinking mindset are essential components of this alignment.

Active participation in professional networks and knowledge-sharing communities amplifies the learning experience. Networking provides exposure to diverse perspectives, industry insights, and collaborative opportunities. Engaging with communities facilitates the exchange of ideas, best practices, and emerging trends, fostering a collective intelligence that transcends individual capabilities. Platforms such as online forums, industry conferences, and social media can serve as powerful conduits for knowledge-sharing.

Volunteering for Boundary-Pushing Projects

For those seeking accelerated growth, volunteering for projects that push boundaries and expand skill sets is a transformative strategy. These projects, often beyond one's comfort zone, provide invaluable hands-on experience and foster resilience in the face of challenges. Volunteering is not only an investment in skill diversification but also an opportunity to showcase leadership potential and a willingness to embrace change.

In essence, continuous learning is not a static endeavour but a dynamic and evolving journey. The convergence of personal aspirations, industry trends, professional networks, and boundary-pushing projects forms a holistic approach to learning that transcends the confines of traditional education. As we witness the rapid pace of change, the commitment to continuous learning becomes a compass guiding individuals toward sustained personal and professional growth. It is not merely a response to change but a proactive strategy to thrive amidst the uncertainties of tomorrow's industries. So, embrace the journey of perpetual learning, for therein lies the key to unlocking your full potential in the ever-evolving landscape of professional possibilities.

A true leader has the
confidence to stand alone,
the courage to make
tough decisions, and the
compassion to listen to
the needs of others.

Chapter 4

Key Leadership Skills
For Aspiring Managers

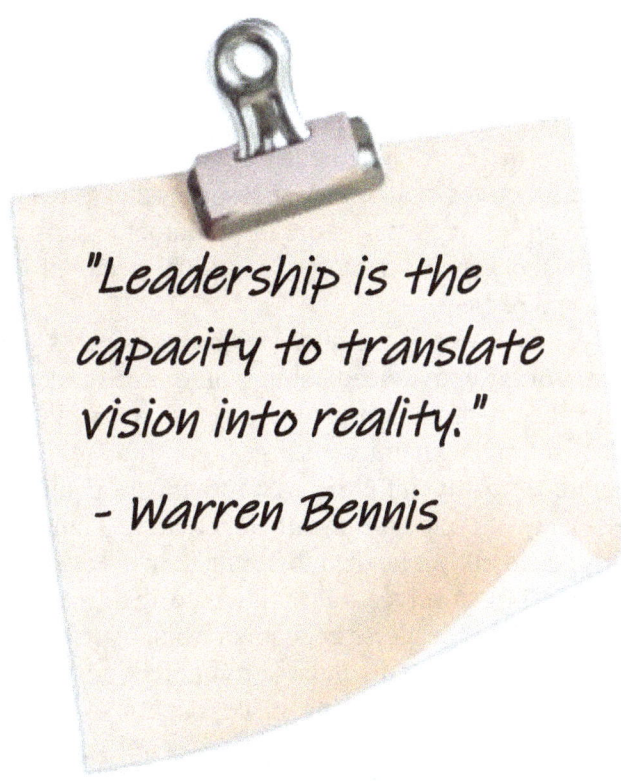

"Leadership is the capacity to translate vision into reality."

- Warren Bennis

Effective communication is the cornerstone of successful leadership, serving as the linchpin that connects leaders with their teams and facilitates the achievement of common goals. Leaders who communicate with assertiveness, clarity, and empathy not only foster a positive and collaborative work environment but also inspire trust and confidence among their team members. Assertiveness in communication involves expressing thoughts, ideas, and expectations clearly and confidently without being overly aggressive or passive. It allows leaders to convey their vision and expectations while maintaining open lines of communication. Clarity is equally paramount, as it ensures that the message is understood precisely, minimizing the risk of misunderstandings or confusion. Leaders must straightforwardly articulate their thoughts, avoiding ambiguity and providing a clear roadmap for the team to follow. Clear communication sets expectations, aligns objectives, and enables everyone to work towards a common purpose. Moreover, leaders should recognize the importance of empathy in their communication style. Empathy involves understanding and sharing the feelings of others, fostering a supportive and inclusive atmosphere. Assertiveness, clarity, and empathy are foundational components of effective communication for leaders, each playing a crucial role in shaping a positive and productive work environment.

Assertiveness involves expressing one's thoughts, needs, and expectations in a clear and confident manner without being domineering, or submissive. Assertive leaders convey a sense of self-assurance and decisiveness, which can inspire confidence among team members. This assertive communication style ensures that leaders are able to advocate for their ideas and expectations while still respecting the input of others. It promotes a healthy balance between being open to different perspectives and decisively moving the team towards common objectives.

Clarity in communication is essential for avoiding misunderstandings and ensuring that everyone is on the same page. Leaders must articulate their messages concisely and unambiguously, leaving no room for interpretation. Clear communication establishes a shared understanding of goals, expectations, and strategies, reducing the likelihood of confusion or misalignment within the team. It also facilitates effective decision-making and problem-solving, as team members can work with a clear understanding of their roles and responsibilities.

Empathy is the ability to understand and share the feelings of others, and it is a key component of effective leadership communication. Leaders who demonstrate empathy show genuine concern for the well-being of their team members. This involves actively listening to their concerns, recognizing their achievements, and acknowledging their emotions. By understanding the perspectives and experiences of others, leaders can build trust, foster collaboration, and create a supportive work environment. Empathetic communication also allows leaders to tailor their approach to the individual needs of team members, promoting a culture of inclusivity and respect.

Assertiveness, clarity, and empathy are interwoven components that, when combined, form a powerful framework for effective leadership communication. Leaders who master these elements can inspire their teams, cultivate a positive workplace culture, and navigate the complexities of organizational dynamics with skill and finesse.

Leaders who integrate empathy into their communication approach demonstrate genuine concern for the well-being of their team members, creating a culture of trust and collaboration. This emotional intelligence allows leaders to connect on a personal level, making it easier for team members to express themselves and contribute their best efforts. The pivotal role of effective communication in leadership cannot be overstated. Leaders who embody assertiveness, clarity, and empathy in their communication style create a foundation for a cohesive and high-performing team, driving success and innovation within the organization.

Critical Thinking

Critical thinking is a foundational element in the domain of managerial decision-making, operating as a cognitive framework that enables leaders to analyze, evaluate, and synthesize information. Managers equipped with strong critical thinking skills can navigate the complexities of decision-making with a strategic mindset, ensuring that choices align with organizational goals and contribute to long-term success.

The strategic perspective of problem-solving and decision-making involves a holistic approach to addressing challenges. It requires managers to consider not only the immediate implications of a decision but also its potential consequences over time. This entails anticipating future developments, understanding market dynamics, and aligning decisions with the organization's vision. Critical thinking plays a pivotal role in this process by fostering a deep understanding of the broader context in which decisions are made.

Accurately identifying and defining problems is a crucial aspect of effective decision-making. Critical thinking prompts managers to go beyond surface-level manifestations of an issue and delve into its root causes. This involves a thorough analysis of the problem's scope, its impact on various aspects of the organization, and the underlying factors contributing to its existence. By engaging in this comprehensive analysis, managers can develop a nuanced understanding of the challenges they face, laying the groundwork for strategic problem-solving.

The significance of framing problems for effective analysis is rooted in the idea that how a problem is defined shapes the range of potential solutions. Critical thinking prompts managers to approach problem framing with precision, ensuring that biases or preconceived notions do not limit their perspective. By adopting a systematic and unbiased approach to problem definition, managers can explore a diverse set of solutions and anticipate potential implications. This nuanced framing allows for a more thorough analysis, increasing the likelihood of identifying innovative and effective solutions.

In essence, critical thinking is the driving force behind effective managerial decision-making. It empowers leaders to approach problem-solving strategically, accurately identify and define problems, and frame them in a way that facilitates in-depth analysis. In doing so, managers enhance their ability to make informed, forward-thinking decisions that contribute to the overall success and sustainability of the organization.

Discovering problem-solving and decision-making from a strategic perspective involves setting the stage for a comprehensive, forward-thinking approach that aligns with the overarching goals and vision of the organization. This strategic lens requires managers to move beyond immediate concerns and consider the long-term implications of their decisions. Here's how to set the stage for strategic problem-solving and decision-making:

1. **Alignment with Organizational Goals:** Begin by aligning problem-solving and decision-making efforts with the broader goals and objectives of the organization. Understand how each decision contributes to the overall mission and vision. This alignment ensures that strategic decisions are not made in isolation but are integral to the organization's trajectory.

2. **Environmental Analysis:** Conduct a thorough analysis of the external and internal business environment. Understand market trends, competitive landscapes, and any potential disruptors. Recognizing the broader context in which decisions are made allows for more informed and adaptive problem-solving. This environmental scan provides the necessary insights to make decisions that are not only effective in the present but also resilient to future changes.

3. **Stakeholder Consideration:** Identify and analyze the various stakeholders affected by the decision-making process. This includes internal teams, customers, suppliers, and regulatory bodies. Understanding the interests and concerns of different stakeholders helps in crafting decisions that balance competing priorities and garner support.

4. **Risk Assessment:** Adopt a risk-aware mindset by assessing potential risks and uncertainties associated with different decision options. This proactive approach allows for the development of risk mitigation strategies and ensures that decisions are made with a clear understanding of potential challenges.

5. **Long-Term Impact Evaluation:** Evaluate the potential long-term impact of each decision. Consider not only the immediate outcomes but also how choices will influence the organization's trajectory over time. This forward-thinking perspective is essential for strategic decision-making that contributes to sustained success.

6. **Data-Driven Insights:** Utilize data and analytics to inform decision-making. A strategic perspective involves relying on factual information and insights to guide choices. Data-driven decision-making enhances the accuracy and effectiveness of problem-solving by providing a solid foundation for strategic thinking.

7. **Continuous Learning and Adaptation:** Embrace a culture of continuous learning and adaptation. Recognize that the strategic landscape is dynamic, and decisions made today may need adjustment in the future. Foster a mindset that encourages learning from both successes and failures, promoting a culture of continuous improvement.

Accurately identifying and defining problems is an art that requires a nuanced and systematic approach. Begin by cultivating a problem-solving mindset that sees challenges as opportunities for improvement. Clearly define the scope of the issue, distinguishing between what the problem is and what it is not. Ask probing questions to explore various dimensions and gather relevant data to ensure a comprehensive understanding. Consider multiple perspectives, recognizing that stakeholders may perceive the problem differently.

Differentiate between symptoms and root causes, addressing the underlying factors for a sustainable solution. Utilize problem-solving tools and methodologies to provide structure to the analysis. Encourage collaboration among diverse stakeholders to enrich the problem definition process. Define measurable outcomes to track progress and objectively evaluate solutions.

Finally, emphasize that problem identification is an iterative process, requiring continuous refinement as new information emerges or solutions are implemented. This holistic approach ensures a thorough and accurate understanding of the problem, laying the foundation for effective and targeted solutions. The significance of framing problems in a way that enables effective analysis cannot be overstated, as the manner in which a problem is defined profoundly influences the subsequent decision-making and solution-finding processes. How a problem is framed sets the boundaries for analysis, shaping the perspectives considered and the range of potential solutions explored.

A precise and well-crafted problem frame not only aids in identifying relevant information but also ensures a more targeted and strategic analysis. It helps to prevent cognitive biases, guiding analysts to approach the problem with an open mind. Moreover, a carefully framed problem provides clarity on the goals and objectives of the analysis, allowing for a focused and efficient use of resources.

The process of framing problems is intricately linked to problem-solving success, as it lays the groundwork for a thorough examination and paves the way for innovative and effective solutions. In essence, the significance of framing problems lies in its power to guide and shape the analytical process, steering it toward a comprehensive and insightful understanding that forms the basis for informed decision-making.

Emotional Intelligence

Emotional intelligence (EI) plays a complex and intricate role in developing strong leadership skills. One crucial aspect involves self-awareness, where leaders with high EI are attuned to their own emotions, strengths, and weaknesses. This self-awareness allows them to regulate their emotions effectively, preventing impulsive decision-making and promoting a calm and collected demeanor even in challenging situations. Additionally, leaders with strong emotional intelligence exhibit a high degree of social awareness, enabling them to empathize with the feelings and perspectives of their team members.

The ability to empathize is a cornerstone of emotional intelligence. Leaders who can understand and share the emotions of others foster a sense of connection and camaraderie within their teams. This empathetic understanding forms the basis for effective communication, conflict resolution, and collaboration. Leaders with high EI can navigate interpersonal dynamics with finesse, addressing conflicts diplomatically and motivating their teams with a genuine understanding of individual needs and aspirations.

Furthermore, emotional intelligence plays a pivotal role in relationship management, the fourth component of EI. Leaders skilled in relationship management can build and maintain strong connections with team members, stakeholders, and peers. They excel in communication, actively listen to feedback, and adapt their leadership style to different personalities and situations. This adaptability contributes to a positive and inclusive organizational culture, enhancing team morale and overall performance.

Components of Emotional Intelligence

1. **Self-Awareness:** Self-awareness is the foundation of emotional intelligence. It involves recognizing and understanding one's own emotions, strengths, weaknesses, values, and motivations. Leaders who are self-aware have a clear understanding of how their emotions impact their behaviour and decision-making. This awareness enables them to leverage their strengths, mitigate potential pitfalls, and foster a genuine authenticity in their leadership approach.

2. **Self-Regulation:** Building on self-awareness, self-regulation is the ability to manage and control one's emotions effectively. Leaders with strong self-regulation skills can remain composed and rational in stressful situations, avoiding impulsive reactions. This emotional control allows leaders to think more clearly, make informed decisions, and maintain a consistent and steady demeanour, even in challenging circumstances.

3. **Social Awareness:** Social awareness involves perceiving and understanding the emotions of others. Leaders with high social awareness are empathetic and attuned to the feelings and needs of their team members. This skill enables leaders to navigate interpersonal dynamics, demonstrate genuine care for their team, and create a supportive and inclusive work environment. Social awareness is crucial for effective communication, conflict resolution, and team collaboration.

4. **Relationship Management:** Relationship management is the outward expression of emotional intelligence. It encompasses the ability to build and maintain positive relationships with others. Leaders skilled in relationship management excel in communication, active listening, and conflict resolution. They can adapt their leadership style to different personalities, motivate their teams, and foster a collaborative and cohesive work culture. Effective relationship management is key to creating a high-performing team and achieving organizational goals.

Recognizing and understanding one's own emotions holds profound significance in personal and professional development. This self-awareness forms the bedrock of emotional intelligence, providing a crucial foundation for various aspects of life. In decision-making, self-awareness enables individuals to navigate choices with a clear understanding of how emotions may influence thoughts and actions, promoting strategic and values-aligned decisions. Effective communication also hinges on self-awareness, allowing individuals to express themselves authentically and foster open dialogue. Moreover, self-awareness plays a pivotal role in stress management, helping individuals identify and cope with stressors to maintain emotional well-being.

In relationships, understanding one's emotions enhances empathy and promotes meaningful connections, contributing to a positive and collaborative social environment. Finally, self-awareness serves as a catalyst for continuous personal growth, empowering individuals to recognize areas for improvement, leverage strengths, and embark on a journey of ongoing development. For leaders, this ability to recognize and understand their own emotions is fundamental to effective leadership, creating an atmosphere conducive to both personal and organizational success.

Self-Awareness Exercises

Journaling	Exercise: Set aside time each day to journal about your thoughts, emotions, and experiences. Reflect on significant events, your reactions, and any patterns you notice.
Mindfulness Meditation	Exercise: Practice mindfulness meditation regularly. Focus on your breath, observe your thoughts without judgment, and notice how your body responds to different emotions.
Strengths and Weaknesses Assessment	Exercise: Make a list of your strengths and weaknesses. Consider how these qualities manifest in different aspects of your life. Reflect on how you can leverage your strengths and address your weaknesses.
Feedback Seeking	Exercise: Ask for feedback from friends, family, or colleagues about your communication style, behavior, or any other aspect you want to understand better. Use this feedback for self-reflection.
Values Clarification	Exercise: Identify your core values. Reflect on whether your actions align with these values and how they contribute to your sense of purpose and fulfillment.
Emotional Journaling	Exercise: Create an emotional journal where you log your emotions throughout the day. Note the triggers and circumstances that evoke specific emotions and analyze recurring patterns.
Timeline of Life Events	Exercise: Create a timeline of significant life events, both positive and challenging. Reflect on how these events have shaped your values, beliefs, and current mindset.
360-Degree Feedback	Exercise: Seek feedback from various sources, including peers, superiors, and subordinates. Compare this feedback to your own self-perception to identify any gaps.
Daily Reflection Questions	Reflection Prompts: • What went well today, and how did it make me feel? • What challenges did I face, and how did I respond emotionally? • How did my interactions with others impact my mood? • Did my actions align with my values today? • What could I do differently in similar situations in the future?
Visual Self-Reflection	Exercise: Create a visual representation of yourself using drawings, symbols, or images that represent different aspects of your identity. Reflect on the meaning behind each element.

Real World Examples
Satya Nadella (CEO of Microsoft)
Satya Nadella is often cited as an example of a leader with high self-awareness. Upon becoming Microsoft's CEO, he emphasized the importance of empathy and emotional intelligence in leadership. He openly discussed his own leadership journey, acknowledging the need for cultural transformation within the organization. His ability to reflect on his own experiences and recognize the need for change has contributed to Microsoft's renewed success.

Sheryl Sandberg (Former COO of Facebook)
Sheryl Sandberg is known for her advocacy of women's leadership and her book "Lean In." After the sudden death of her husband, Sandberg publicly shared her personal challenges and grief. This level of vulnerability and openness demonstrates a high degree of self-awareness. Sandberg uses her experiences to connect with others, fostering empathy and resilience.

Warren Buffett (CEO of Berkshire Hathaway)
Warren Buffett, one of the most successful investors in the world, is recognized for his humility and self-awareness. Despite his immense wealth and success, Buffett remains down-to-earth and acknowledges his own mistakes. He openly discusses his investment blunders, emphasizing the importance of learning from failures. This transparency and humility contribute to his enduring reputation as a wise and respected leader.

Brene Brown (Researcher and Author)
Brene Brown, a researcher on vulnerability and shame, demonstrates high levels of self-awareness through her work. In her TED Talks and books, she shares personal stories and reflections on her own struggles, creating a connection with her audience. Brown's ability to articulate her vulnerabilities and embrace imperfection contributes to her influence as a thought leader on topics related to human connection and resilience.

Tim Cook (CEO of Apple)
Tim Cook has shown self-awareness by openly discussing his experience as a leader and addressing challenges faced by Apple, such as issues related to diversity and environmental sustainability. Cook has also been vocal about his leadership style, emphasizing the importance of empathy and collaboration. His self-awareness contributes to a corporate culture that values inclusivity and innovation.

Note to Yourself

Dear Esteemed Leaders,

In the symphony of leadership, let motivation be the loud melody that echoes through every endeavor. As you stand at the wheel of inspiration, envision a future where each challenge becomes an opportunity, and every setback is a stepping stone toward greatness. Your intrinsic motivation is the magnetic force that draws others toward shared aspirations; let it be the catalyst for transformative change.

Amid the dynamic landscape of leadership, emotional intelligence emerges as your guiding star. In the intricate dance of human connection, the ability to navigate emotions with empathy and understanding is your greatest asset. Listen not just to words but to the unspoken nuances of feelings, fostering a culture where compassion is the currency and collaboration is the natural rhythm.

In the quiet corridors of self-reflection, let self-awareness be the torch that illuminates your path. Acknowledge your strengths, for they are the pillars of your leadership, and embrace your vulnerabilities, for they are the stepping stones to growth. As you traverse the landscape of self-discovery, recognize

Chapter 5

From Vision to Mentality
"Cultivating a Managerial Mindset"

Task-Focused

Being task-focused involves directing one's attention primarily toward the specific activities and assignments that need to be completed. Individuals who are task-focused are meticulous about the steps and processes required to accomplish immediate responsibilities. Their focus is on the execution of individual tasks with precision and efficiency. While this approach ensures that work is completed with attention to detail, it may sometimes lead to a narrow focus, potentially overlooking the broader objectives or long-term outcomes.

Goal-Oriented

On the other hand, being goal-oriented involves a broader perspective that goes beyond the completion of individual tasks. Goal-oriented individuals are driven by overarching objectives, targets, or outcomes. They align their tasks with larger goals, ensuring that each activity contributes meaningfully to the overall vision. This approach encourages a strategic mindset, emphasizing the importance of understanding the purpose behind tasks and how they fit into the larger picture. While goal-oriented individuals are mindful of tasks, they prioritize them based on their impact on the achievement of broader objectives.

A purely task-focused approach, while effective in managing specific activities, comes with inherent limitations that can hinder overall effectiveness and goal attainment.

1. **Lack of Strategic Vision:** A purely task-focused approach may result in a lack of strategic vision. Individuals may become so engrossed in the details of immediate tasks that they lose sight of the broader goals and objectives. This tunnel vision can hinder the alignment of tasks with the organization's overarching mission and long-term vision.

2. **Reduced Adaptability:** Task-focused individuals may find it challenging to adapt to changes or unexpected developments. Since their attention is primarily on the completion of specific tasks, they may struggle to pivot or adjust strategies when circumstances evolve. This lack of adaptability can hinder resilience in dynamic and unpredictable environments.

3. **Potential Burnout:** Constantly focusing on tasks without considering the bigger picture can lead to burnout. Task-focused individuals may feel overwhelmed by the volume of immediate responsibilities, especially if there is little consideration for the impact on personal well-being or work-life balance.

4. **Limited Innovation and Creativity:** A purely task-oriented mindset may stifle innovation and creativity. Individuals may become overly fixated on routine and established procedures, neglecting opportunities for novel approaches or improvements. Creativity often thrives when there is room for exploration beyond the confines of specific tasks.

5. **Missed Opportunities for Collaboration:** Task-focused individuals may be less inclined to collaborate effectively. Since their primary focus is on completing assigned tasks, they might overlook opportunities to engage with others, share insights, or collaborate on projects that could lead to more comprehensive and innovative solutions.

6. **Potential for Micromanagement:** A task-focused mindset, if not balanced appropriately, can lead to micromanagement. Individuals may become overly concerned with the minutiae of tasks, potentially stifling autonomy and creativity among team members. This can negatively impact morale and hinder a collaborative work environment.

7. **Short-Term Focus at the Expense of Long-Term Goals:** A sole emphasis on tasks may lead to a short-term focus at the expense of long-term goals. While tasks are completed efficiently, the overall strategic direction and sustainable growth of the organization might be compromised.

A goal-oriented mindset goes beyond the routine completion of tasks....

A goal-oriented mindset goes beyond the routine completion of tasks, investigating a broader perspective rooted in strategic thinking and forward-looking vision. At its core, being goal-oriented involves a deep commitment to aligning every action with the overarching objectives of an organization or individual.

Those with this mindset actively seek to comprehend the strategic direction and long-term vision, recognizing that immediate tasks are interconnected building blocks that pave the way for the realization of larger, enduring goals. Strategic thinking is a fundamental element where individuals engage in meticulous planning and decision-making, considering the broader implications of their actions on the organizational strategy.

This involves assessing risks, anticipating challenges, and making informed choices that contribute to the achievement of strategic milestones. A goal-oriented approach is characterized by a focus on the long-term vision, emphasizing sustainability and resilience. Flexibility is also inherent, as goal-oriented individuals understand that goals may evolve, requiring adaptability in strategies and tactics while maintaining alignment with the overarching vision.

Moreover, being goal-oriented entails an outcome-oriented focus, where every task is seen as a meaningful contribution to specific, measurable, and impactful goals. Resource allocation and prioritization are guided by strategic thinking, ensuring that efforts are concentrated where they can have the most significant impact.

Collaboration and effective communication become integral components, recognizing that shared objectives are best achieved through collective effort and a cohesive team. In essence, being goal-oriented embodies a comprehensive, strategic, and future-oriented mindset that not only enhances individual effectiveness but also fosters the overall success and sustainability of the organization.

Operational and Strategic Thinking

Operational thinking and strategic thinking represent contrasting paradigms in organizational decision-making. Operational thinking is characterized by a short-term focus, centring on the day-to-day tasks and activities that ensure the efficient execution of established processes. It pertains to lower levels of management, emphasizing consistency and adherence to established procedures. In contrast, strategic thinking adopts a long-term perspective concerned with shaping the overall direction and goals of the organization.

This approach involves a comprehensive analysis of the external environment, market trends, and the organization's strengths and weaknesses. Strategic decisions, often made by top-level executives, are pivotal in navigating complex challenges and opportunities that could significantly impact the organization's competitive position and success. While operational thinking prioritizes the immediate problems and efficiencies within the existing framework, strategic thinking requires flexibility, adaptability, and a focus on future outcomes.

The metrics and measurements also differ, with operational thinking often relying on short-term, quantifiable metrics, while strategic thinking considers a broader set of indicators related to long-term organizational health and success. Both operational and strategic thinking are integral to organizational success, each playing a crucial role in navigating the intricacies of day-to-day operations and steering the organization toward its future vision.

Operational thinking is inherently reactive, responding to immediate needs and concerns within the existing framework of day-to-day operations. It is characterized by a focus on routine tasks, efficiency, and the execution of established procedures. This reactive nature is evident in the way operational decisions are often made in response to the challenges and demands of the moment, aiming to resolve immediate issues and ensure the smooth functioning of ongoing processes.

On the other hand, strategic thinking stands in stark contrast with its proactive and forward-looking orientation. Strategic thinking involves a deliberate and comprehensive approach to decision-making that goes beyond reacting to current circumstances. It requires anticipation of future challenges and opportunities, considering the long-term vision of the organization. Strategic decisions are not made solely in response to existing problems but are shaped by a proactive analysis of the external environment, market trends, and the organization's internal capabilities.

Proactive strategic thinking involves envisioning and planning for the future, identifying potential trends, and positioning the organization to capitalize on emerging opportunities. It requires a willingness to adapt to changing circumstances and a commitment to innovation and continuous improvement. Rather than simply addressing immediate concerns, strategic thinking aims to shape the destiny of the organization, setting a course for long-term success and sustainability.

However, while operational thinking reacts to the demands of the present, strategic thinking takes a proactive stance, guiding the organization towards a future vision. This dichotomy underscores the need for a balanced approach, where both reactive and proactive thinking contribute harmoniously to an organization's overall effectiveness and resilience.

Change Management

Change is an inherent and inevitable aspect of organizational life, driven by factors such as technological advancements, market dynamics, competitive pressures, and internal organizational goals. Understanding the nature of change is crucial for organizations to navigate transitions effectively. Change can manifest in various forms, including structural reorganizations, process improvements, technological adoptions, mergers and acquisitions, and shifts in organizational culture.

The inevitability of change in organizations is rooted in the dynamic nature of the business environment. External forces, such as economic fluctuations and advancements in technology, continuously reshape industries, necessitating organizational responses. Internally, organizations evolve to meet new challenges, capitalize on emerging opportunities, and adapt to shifting customer preferences. In this context, organizations that recognize change as a constant and embrace a proactive approach are better positioned to thrive in dynamic environments.

The reactive and proactive approaches to change represent two distinct mindsets and strategies in dealing with organizational transitions:

1. Reactive Approach:

- **Nature:** The reactive approach to change is characterized by responding to changes as they occur or after they have already taken place. Organizations adopting a reactive stance may wait until external pressures or internal issues force them to make adjustments.

- **Response to Events:** Reactive organizations tend to respond to specific events, crises, or challenges rather than anticipating and preparing for them. Decisions are made in response to immediate needs, often in a hurried or crisis-driven manner.

- **Risk of Resistance:** The reactive approach may face resistance from employees who feel unprepared for changes, leading to potential disruptions in productivity and morale. Communication about changes may be perceived as insufficient or lacking transparency.

- **Limited Strategic Alignment:** Reactive changes may lack alignment with the overall strategic goals of the organization, resulting in a series of disjointed adjustments rather than a cohesive, purposeful transformation.

2. Proactive Approach:

- **Nature:** The proactive approach involves anticipating and initiating changes before they become imperative. Proactive organizations actively seek opportunities for improvement, innovation, and adaptation to stay ahead of the curve.

- **Strategic Planning:** Proactive organizations engage in strategic planning that considers future scenarios, industry trends, and potential disruptions. This approach allows for the identification of opportunities and challenges in advance.

- **Employee Involvement:** Proactive change involves engaging employees in the change process, fostering a culture of continuous improvement, and providing them with the tools and mindset to adapt to evolving circumstances.

- **Strategic Alignment:** Proactive changes are more likely to align with the organization's strategic goals, ensuring that adaptations contribute to long-term success and sustainability.

- **Reduced Resistance:** Proactive organizations may experience less resistance to change as employees are better prepared, informed, and involved in the decision-making process.

Cultivating a culture that wholeheartedly embraces change is paramount for organizations seeking sustained success and adaptability in today's dynamic business landscape. Such a culture instils adaptability and resilience at all levels, enabling individuals and teams to navigate uncertainties, respond adeptly to challenges, and flourish amid constant change. Moreover, a change-embracing culture fosters innovation and creativity, encouraging employees to contribute novel ideas and solutions that drive continuous improvement. Organizations with such cultures gain a competitive advantage by staying ahead of market shifts, technological advancements, and evolving customer preferences. Beyond its external impact, a culture that welcomes change significantly influences internal dynamics, enhancing employee engagement and morale. When employees feel empowered to contribute to positive transformations, they become more motivated, satisfied, and committed to the organization's overall success. This cultural attribute becomes a magnet for top talent, attracting forward-thinking individuals who seek environments that encourage growth, learning, and meaningful contributions. Furthermore, a change-embracing culture facilitates the organization's ability to respond to shifting customer needs and expectations, ensuring sustained relevance and customer satisfaction. It also aligns organizational changes with strategic goals, fostering a shared understanding of the purpose behind initiatives and garnering widespread support. In terms of risk management, a culture that values change allows organizations to proactively

identify and respond to potential challenges, minimizing the impact of unexpected events and maintaining operational stability. This culture is inherently inclined toward continuous improvement, encouraging individuals to assess existing processes, identify inefficiencies, and seek opportunities for enhancement. Ultimately, an organizational culture that embraces change fosters agility, allowing the organization to pivot swiftly, capitalize on emerging opportunities, and effectively navigate complex and dynamic environments. In essence, it becomes the bedrock for sustained success, driving innovation, talent attraction, and strategic resilience.

The connection between innovation, continuous improvement, and proactive change is integral to organizational success, fostering a dynamic environment that adapts to evolving circumstances. Organizations that prioritize innovation are inherently better equipped to drive proactive change and embrace a culture of continuous improvement.

Innovation serves as a catalyst for change by introducing novel ideas, technologies, and approaches. When organizations foster a culture of innovation, they encourage employees to think creatively, challenge the status quo, and explore new solutions to existing challenges. This proactive approach to problem-solving is closely linked to the concept of continuous improvement, where organizations continuously seek to enhance processes, products, and services.

Continuous improvement, often associated with methodologies like Lean or Six Sigma, involves an ongoing effort to identify inefficiencies, streamline processes, and optimize performance. This mindset aligns with innovation, as both concepts share the goal of seeking better ways of doing things. The synergy between innovation and continuous improvement creates a fertile ground for proactive change as organizations seek opportunities to evolve and stay ahead of the curve.

Organizations prioritizing innovation are likely to be early adopters of emerging trends and technologies. This forward-thinking approach positions them as leaders rather than followers in their industries. When new challenges or opportunities arise, these organizations are primed to proactively initiate change, leveraging their innovative capacity to navigate uncertainties and capitalize on emerging trends.

Moreover, a culture of innovation fosters a mindset of adaptability and resilience. Employees in innovative organizations are more open to change, as they are accustomed to experimenting with new ideas and approaches. This adaptability is crucial in a rapidly changing business environment, where organizations must be agile and responsive to stay competitive.

The link between innovation, continuous improvement, and proactive change lies in their shared emphasis on seeking improvement and embracing new ideas. Organizations that prioritize innovation are better equipped to drive proactive change because they have instilled

a culture that encourages creativity, embraces experimentation, and values the continuous pursuit of better outcomes. This synergy creates a positive feedback loop, where innovation begets continuous improvement, which, in turn, fuels a proactive approach to change, ultimately contributing to organizational success and sustainability.

Chapter **6**
Building Bridges - Developing Managerial Skills in Your Current Role

Problem-Solving Methods

Design Thinking

Design thinking is a human-centred approach emphasizing empathy, ideation, and prototyping. It encourages a deep understanding of end-users and their needs, fostering creative solutions that resonate with the intended audience.

Brainstorming

A classic but powerful method, brainstorming brings together diverse perspectives to generate many ideas. Encouraging a free flow of thoughts without immediate evaluation stimulates creativity, often leading to unexpected and innovative solutions.

Mind Mapping

Mind mapping is a visual technique that helps organize thoughts and ideas hierarchically and interconnectedly. It promotes creative thinking by allowing individuals or teams to explore associations and relationships among different problem elements.

SCAMPER Technique

SCAMPER stands for Substitute, Combine, Adapt, Modify, Put to another use, Eliminate, and Reverse. This technique encourages individuals to explore different dimensions of a problem by considering how it can be modified or transformed using these seven approaches.

TRIZ (Theory of Inventive Problem Solving)

TRIZ is a systematic problem-solving method that originated in Russia. It provides a structured approach for analyzing and solving technical problems by leveraging inventive principles and identifying contradictions in the problem space.

Six Thinking Hats

Developed by Edward de Bono, the Six Thinking Hats method assigns individuals or groups different thinking modes (creativity, critical thinking, and optimism). This helps in exploring a problem from multiple perspectives and fostering innovative solutions.

Prototyping

Prototyping involves creating a simplified, tangible representation of a solution. It allows for hands-on exploration and testing, facilitating the identification of potential improvements and innovations before full implementation.

Reverse Thinking

In reverse thinking, individuals approach a problem by considering the opposite of the conventional solutions. This inversion technique often leads to fresh perspectives and innovative insights by challenging traditional assumptions.

Hackathons and Innovation Challenges

Creating events like hackathons or innovation challenges provides a platform for individuals or teams to tackle specific problems collaboratively within a constrained timeframe. These formats often yield creative and innovative solutions driven by competition and collaboration.

Cross-Functional Collaboration

Bringing together individuals from diverse backgrounds and expertise areas fosters cross-pollination of ideas. Cross-functional collaboration ensures that a problem is approached from various angles, encouraging innovation by integrating different perspectives.

Tycoon Creative Problem-Solving Methods

Netflix disrupted the traditional entertainment industry by creatively addressing the challenge of content distribution. Its shift from a DVD rental model to a streaming platform and data-driven content recommendations demonstrate how the company applied innovative thinking to transform how people consume entertainment.

 P&G is known for its Connect + Develop program, which encourages open innovation. By collaborating with external partners, P&G seeks creative solutions to product development challenges. This approach has led to successful products like the Swiffer and the Gillette Fusion razor.

Tesla, led by Elon Musk, is known for its innovative approaches to address challenges in the automotive industry. The development of electric vehicles, the Gigafactory for sustainable energy production, and advancements in autonomous driving technology reflect Tesla's commitment to creative problem-solving and pushing technological frontiers.

Google's commitment to fostering a culture of innovation is evident in projects like Google X, the company's experimental research division. Initiatives like Google Glass, self-driving cars, and Project Loon (providing internet access via high-altitude balloons) showcase the  application of creative problem-solving to push the boundaries of technology.

Taking initiative-Seeing and Seizing Opportunities for Improvement

Taking the initiative is a proactive and self-driven approach to personal and professional endeavours, characterized by a willingness to assume responsibility, identify opportunities, and initiate actions without explicit instructions. Individuals who take the initiative demonstrate a forward-thinking mindset, actively seeking ways to contribute positively to their environment. This involves anticipating challenges and opportunities and proactively addressing them rather than waiting for external cues.

Taking the initiative requires a clear understanding of one's goals and a commitment to making tangible contributions towards their achievement. It involves a bias towards action, a readiness to step into leadership roles, and an ability to navigate uncertainty effectively. Initiators identify areas for improvement and take decisive steps to implement positive change. This proactive stance is rooted in ownership and accountability, with individuals recognizing that their actions are crucial in driving personal, team, or organizational success.

Effective communication, resilience in the face of challenges, and a continuous learning orientation are integral facets of taking initiative, contributing to a dynamic and impactful approach to personal and professional growth.

The Stages for Reconnoitering the Mindset of Proactive Individuals

Stage 1

Anticipation and Awareness

The first stage involves recognizing the importance of anticipation and awareness in proactive individuals. Proactive individuals display a heightened sense of foresight, actively scanning their environment for potential opportunities and challenges. They possess a keen understanding of industry trends, market shifts, and emerging developments, allowing them to stay ahead of the curve.

Stage 2

Initiative and Action Orientation

Building on anticipation, the second stage centers on proactive individuals' initiative and action-oriented nature. They don't merely identify opportunities or challenges; they take decisive steps to initiate positive change. This stage involves understanding the proactive mindset's core principle: the willingness to take ownership and act without waiting for explicit instructions.

Stage 3

Solution-Oriented Thinking

Proactive individuals exhibit a distinctive approach to problem-solving. In this stage, the focus is on their solution-oriented thinking. Rather than being overwhelmed by challenges, they channel their energy into finding viable solutions. This involves creative problem-solving, a commitment to overcoming obstacles, and a belief that their actions can contribute to positive outcomes.

Stage 4

Continuous Learning and Adaptability

The fourth stage delves into the proactive mindset's continuous learning and adaptability aspect. Proactive individuals recognize the importance of ongoing personal and professional development. They actively seek opportunities to expand their knowledge, acquire new skills, and stay adaptable in the face of evolving circumstances.

Stage 5

Resilience and Growth Mindset

Proactive individuals demonstrate resilience when confronted with setbacks. This stage involves understanding how they view challenges as opportunities for growth. Rather than being discouraged by failures, they extract valuable lessons, adjust their approach, and move forward with a growth mindset that fuels their ongoing development.

Stage 6

Ownership and Accountability

The stage of ownership and accountability is crucial in understanding the proactive mindset. Proactive individuals take responsibility for their actions and outcomes. This involves a deep sense of ownership, where they recognize the impact of their efforts on projects, teams, or organizational success, fostering a culture of accountability.

Stage 7

Effective Time Management

The seventh stage explores how proactive individuals excel in time management. They prioritize tasks and activities strategically, maximizing their impact. This stage involves recognizing the importance of setting goals, creating action plans, and efficiently allocating resources to achieve desired outcomes.

Stage 8

Clear Communication

In the final stage, attention is given to the role of clear communication in the proactive mindset. Proactive individuals effectively communicate their ideas, initiatives, and concerns to stakeholders. This ensures that others know their intentions, fostering collaboration and garnering support for bold endeavours.

Characteristics of individuals who actively Seek and Capitalize on Opportunities

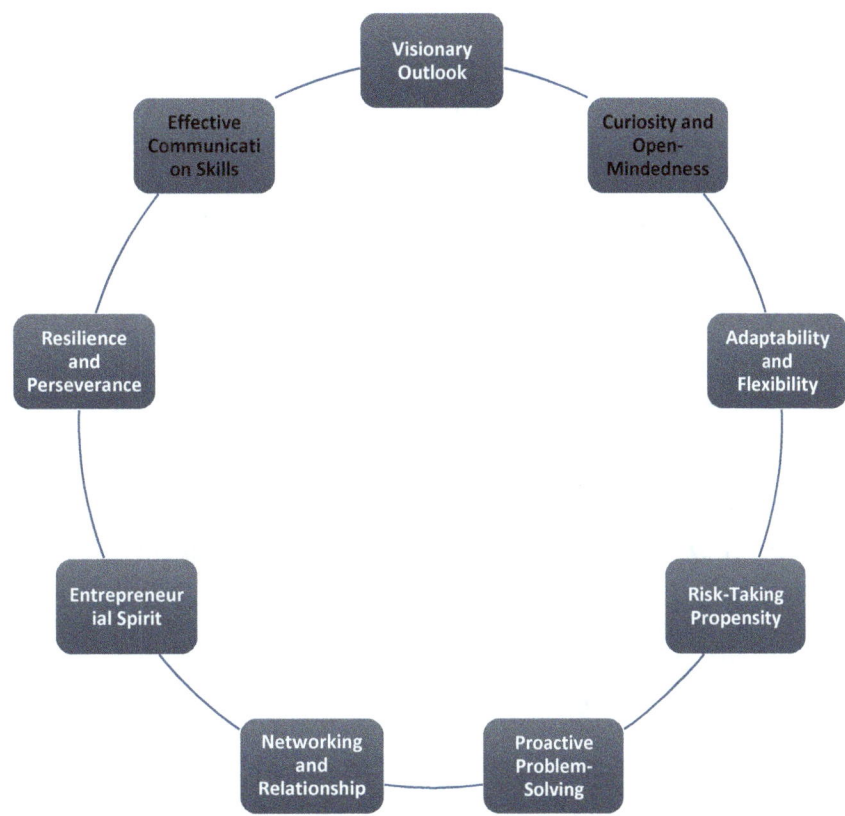

Examples of Common Situations

IT Department

Legacy System Upgrades: IT professionals may recognize opportunities for improvement when dealing with outdated legacy systems. Identifying and advocating for upgrading or replacing legacy systems can enhance efficiency, security, and overall system performance.

Human Resources Department

Employee Onboarding Process: HR professionals might identify opportunities for improvement in the employee onboarding process. Streamlining paperwork, incorporating digital tools, and enhancing the orientation experience can lead to a more seamless and engaging onboarding process.

Marketing Department

Social Media Engagement: Marketing professionals may recognize opportunities for improvement in social media engagement. Analyzing data on audience interactions, identifying peak engagement times, and adjusting content strategies can optimize social media campaigns and enhance brand visibility.

Finance Department

Expense Management: Finance professionals might identify opportunities for improvement in expense management. Implementing digital expense tracking systems, conducting regular audits, and negotiating better vendor contracts can reduce costs and improve financial efficiency.

Customer Support Department

Response Time Improvement: Customer support teams can identify opportunities for improvement in response times to customer queries. Implementing ticketing systems, optimizing workflow processes, and providing additional training can lead to quicker and more effective customer support.

Sales Department

Sales Funnel Optimization: Sales professionals may recognize opportunities for improvement in the sales funnel. Analyzing customer touchpoints, refining sales pitches, and providing additional training to sales representatives can enhance conversion rates and overall sales performance.

Research and Development Department

Innovation Processes: R&D teams might identify opportunities for improvement in innovation processes. Encouraging cross-functional collaboration, implementing idea management platforms, and allocating dedicated time for creative thinking can foster a culture of innovation.

Supply Chain Management Department

Inventory Optimization: Professionals in supply chain management can identify opportunities for improvement in inventory management. Implementing data-driven forecasting, adopting just-in-time inventory practices, and optimizing order fulfilment processes can lead to cost savings and improved efficiency.

Quality Assurance Department

Process Standardization: Quality assurance professionals might recognize opportunities for improvement in standardizing testing processes. Implementing standardized testing protocols, leveraging automation tools, and conducting regular process reviews can enhance product quality and efficiency.

Legal Department

Contract Management*:* Legal professionals can identify opportunities for improvement in contract management processes. Implementing digital contract repositories, standardizing contract templates, and streamlining approval workflows can improve efficiency and reduce legal risks.

Training and Development Department

Skill Enhancement Programs: Professionals in training and development can identify opportunities for improvement by assessing employee skill gaps. Designing targeted training programs, leveraging e-learning platforms, and conducting regular skills assessments can contribute to employee development and organizational growth.

Passive and Proactive Mindset

A passive mindset is characterized by a reactive approach to life's challenges and opportunities. Individuals with a passive attitude often respond to situations as they unfold, lacking a proactive stance in shaping their circumstances. This mindset is marked by relying on others for guidance and decision-making, waiting for instructions rather than actively seeking opportunities or solutions.

Passivity tends to be associated with risk aversion, as those with this mindset may shy away from taking bold actions or stepping out of their comfort zones. Goal setting in a passive mindset may be limited and undefined, and there's a tendency to blame external factors when challenges arise rather than taking ownership of the situation. The passive mindset is often resistant to change, preferring the familiarity of the status quo and exhibiting a reluctance to embrace new ideas or approaches.

On the other hand, a proactive mindset is characterized by an anticipatory and initiative-taking approach. Individuals with a proactive attitude actively seek opportunities, make decisions, and take steps to shape their destinies. Farsighted individuals do not wait for instructions but actively seek ways to improve situations, contribute positively, and initiate positive change. This mindset is marked by a willingness to take calculated risks and step out of one's comfort zone to pursue growth and improvement. Proactive individuals set clear goals for themselves and take strategic steps to achieve them, demonstrating a sense of ownership and accountability for their actions.

When faced with challenges, a proactive mindset involves problem-solving rather than assigning blame to external factors. Additionally, a proactive attitude embraces change, viewing it as an opportunity for growth and innovation, and actively seeks new ideas and approaches to enhance personal and professional outcomes.

Transitioning from a reactive approach to a proactive mindset necessitates a multifaceted strategy woven with deliberate actions and mindful reflections. As Antoine de Saint-Exupéry stated, *"A goal without a plan is just a wish,"* underlining the essence of clear, strategic goals as the foundational step toward a proactive mindset. These goals should adhere to the SMART criteria—specific, measurable, achievable, relevant, and time-bound—to provide a robust framework for proactive decision-making.

Developing comprehensive action plans stands as the subsequent stage in this transformative journey. Breaking down overarching objectives into manageable tasks and prioritizing them based on urgency and importance fosters a systematic and proactive approach to task execution. In the words of legendary basketball coach John Wooden, *"Don't let what you cannot do interfere with what you can do."* This sentiment echoes the proactive mindset, emphasizing the importance of focusing on actionable tasks within one's control.

Establishing proactive routines further reinforces this shift, carving out dedicated time for strategic thinking, planning, and goal setting. Consistently allocating specific time slots for proactive activities helps ingrain the habit of proactivity into daily life. Pausing to reflect on the insightful words of Peter Drucker, *"The best way to predict the future is to create it,"* inspires the cultivation of a proactive mindset by actively shaping one's destiny through intentional actions.

Anticipating challenges before they arise is a pivotal component of proactivity. This involves developing contingency plans, embracing a forward-thinking mindset, and acknowledging that challenges are inherent in any growth journey. The proactive individual approaches obstacles as opportunities for learning and improvement, echoing the sentiment expressed by Winston S. Churchill: *"The pessimist complains about the wind; the optimist expects it to change; the realist adjusts the sails."*

Continuous learning serves as a cornerstone of the proactive mindset. Remaining informed about industry trends, emerging technologies, and relevant developments empowers individuals to stay ahead of the curve. Albert Einstein's famous words, *"Wisdom is not a product of schooling but of the lifelong attempt to acquire it,"* resonate here, emphasizing the importance of an ongoing commitment to learning.

Taking the initiative emerges as a defining trait of a proactive mindset. Volunteering for new projects, suggesting improvements, and actively seeking opportunities for growth and development characterize individuals who embrace a proactive approach. As Theodore Roosevelt articulated, *"Do what you can, with what you have, where you are,"* embodies the essence of seizing the present moment and taking affirmative action.

Effective time management becomes a practical manifestation of proactivity. Utilizing tools like calendars and to-do lists, prioritizing tasks, and aligning them with overarching goals ensures that time is invested strategically. Recognizing the wisdom in Warren Buffett's words, *"The difference between successful people and successful people is that successful people say no to almost everything,"* underscores the importance of prioritization and focus.

Delegating tasks judiciously is another facet of a proactive mindset. Recognizing when tasks can be entrusted to others allows individuals to concentrate on more strategic and high-impact activities. This aligns with the philosophy captured in John C. Maxwell's statement, *"Leadership is not about being in charge. It's about taking care of those in your charge,"* emphasizing the proactive responsibility of effective delegation.

Cultivating resilience in the face of setbacks is an integral element of proactivity. Viewing challenges as opportunities for growth and learning echoes the sentiment of Henry Ford: *"Failure is simply the opportunity to begin again, this time more intelligently."* Resilience enables individuals to bounce back from setbacks, fostering adaptability and perseverance.

Seeking feedback and engaging in reflective practices contribute to a continuous improvement cycle, reinforcing the shift from reactive to proactive. Individuals ensure an ongoing evolution toward greater proactivity by actively learning from experiences, analyzing patterns, and adjusting strategies accordingly. To quote renowned management guru Peter Drucker, *"Follow effective action with quiet reflection. From the quiet reflection, will come even more effective action,"* encapsulating the cyclical nature of proactive improvement.

Responsibility Expansion

Getting more responsibilities at work is like getting more chances to learn and grow in your job. When your responsibilities expand, it means you get to do new things and face different challenges. This is really good for your career because you get hands-on experience, which is the best way to learn new skills. You might find yourself leading a team or working with people from other parts of the company. This is cool because it helps you become a better leader, improves how you talk to others, and makes you good at solving problems.

Having more to do at work also teaches you to handle tough situations and be flexible when things change. It's like solving puzzles – you learn how to figure out what's going on and find the best solutions. You become a kind of problem-solving expert!

When you take on more responsibilities, you're not just learning technical stuff; you're also becoming better at working with others. You build strong relationships with people in different parts of the company, and this can open up even more opportunities for you. So, getting more responsibilities isn't just about doing more work; it's about learning, growing, and becoming really good at what you do.

Cross-Functional Collaboration

Cross-functional collaboration is a dynamic approach to working within an organization, involving individuals or teams from different departments or functional areas collectively tackling tasks, solving problems, or achieving shared objectives. In the intricate web of a dynamic business environment, the significance of cross-functional collaboration cannot be overstated.

One of its primary values lies in fostering innovation and creativity. By bringing together individuals with diverse backgrounds, skills, and perspectives, cross-functional teams become incubators for fresh ideas and inventive solutions. This diversity injects vitality into problem-solving processes and product development, propelling the organization forward in an ever-evolving market.

Efficient problem-solving is another crucial aspect. Complex challenges often require multifaceted solutions. Cross-functional teams, drawing from the collective knowledge and expertise of members spanning various departments, are better equipped to address intricate issues comprehensively. This collaborative approach ensures that decisions and strategies are not limited by the narrow viewpoint of a single department.

Breaking down silos within an organization is a significant communication advantage. Traditional structures can create barriers between departments, impeding the flow of information. Cross-functional collaboration dismantles these barriers, fostering open communication channels and creating a more interconnected workplace. This improved communication is especially vital in a fast-paced business environment where timely information sharing can be a decisive factor.

In the context of a dynamic business environment, agility and adaptability are key. Cross-functional collaboration enables teams to respond swiftly to changes, whether they are market shifts, emerging trends, or unforeseen challenges. By pooling resources and expertise, organizations become more resilient and better positioned to navigate uncertainties.

Furthermore, cross-functional collaboration provides valuable learning opportunities, contributing to the professional development of team members. Exposure to different skill sets and perspectives broadens individuals' knowledge base, making them more versatile contributors to the organization.

Effective decision-making is another outcome of cross-functional collaboration. When diverse perspectives are considered, decisions are more likely to be well-rounded and reflective of the organization's overarching goals. This holistic decision-making approach strengthens the strategic alignment of initiatives with the broader mission of the company.

Employee engagement is enhanced through cross-functional collaboration as it creates a sense of ownership and shared responsibility. When employees from various departments actively participate in collaborative efforts, they feel a stronger connection to the organization's objectives, fostering a positive work culture.

Moreover, cross-functional collaboration aligns organizational efforts with customer needs. Different functions often hold unique insights into customer preferences and behaviors. Collaborative efforts ensure a more customer-centric approach, aligning products and services with the diverse requirements of the customer base.

Efficiency and resource optimization are achieved through optimal resource utilization. Instead of duplicating efforts, cross-functional teams can share resources, reducing costs and improving overall efficiency.

T-Curve Model Study

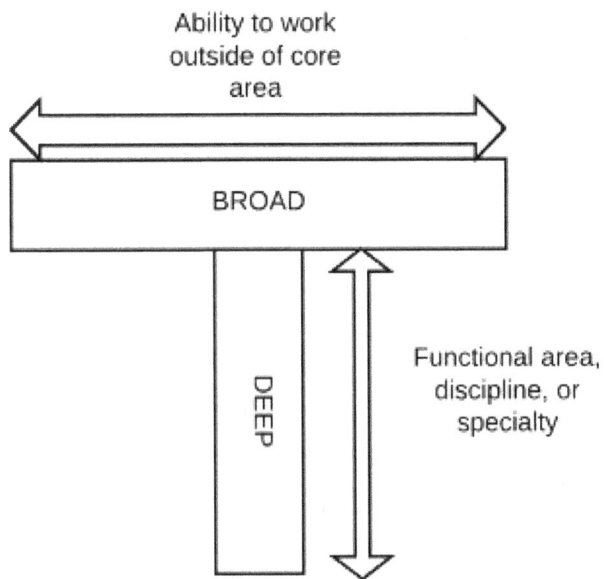

The concept of T-shaped skills represents a unique and effective approach to personal and professional development, envisioning individuals as possessing both depth and breadth of expertise. Imagine the letter "T," where the vertical bar symbolizes deep proficiency in a specific field, while the horizontal bar represents a broader understanding across diverse disciplines. This metaphor encapsulates the essence of cultivating specialized expertise (the vertical bar) while also fostering a versatility that spans multiple domains (the horizontal bar).

At its core, the concept of T-shaped skills advocates for individuals to go beyond mere specialization and embrace a more holistic and interconnected approach to learning and growth. The vertical bar signifies the in-depth knowledge, skills, and mastery within a particular field, showcasing a person's specialization and competence in a specific area. This depth is often the result of focused education, hands-on experience, and continuous refinement of expertise.

In contrast, the horizontal bar embodies the individual's capacity to apply their skills and knowledge across various disciplines, showcasing adaptability, versatility, and a willingness to explore beyond their core specialization. This breadth of understanding allows individuals to communicate effectively with professionals from diverse backgrounds, fostering collaboration and innovation.

Vertical Bar-Deep Expertise

The vertical bar represents an individual's deep expertise in a specific field. This is the "stem" of the T, showcasing in-depth knowledge, skills, and mastery within a particular discipline. Here are key aspects of the vertical bar:

1. **Specialized Knowledge:**
   - **Education and Training:** Acquiring specialized education and training in a specific domain, often through formal education, certifications, or workshops.
   - **Professional Experience:** Gaining hands-on experience and exposure to real-world challenges within the chosen field.

2. **Mastery of Skills:**
   - **Technical Proficiency:** Developing a high level of technical proficiency and skills relevant to the specialized area.
   - **Problem-solving:** Building expertise in solving complex problems and overcoming challenges specific to the chosen field.

3. **Continuous Learning:**
   - **Staying Updated:** Keeping abreast of the latest advancements, trends, and developments within the specialized domain through continuous learning and professional development.

Horizontal Bar-Breadth of Knowledge

The horizontal bar signifies the individual's capacity to apply their skills and knowledge across various disciplines. It represents adaptability, versatility, and a willingness to explore beyond the core specialization. Here are key aspects of the horizontal bar:

1. **Interdisciplinary Understanding:**
   - **Cross-functional Awareness:** Developing an understanding of how different functions and disciplines within an organization operate.
   - **Interconnected Knowledge:** Bridging the gap between the specialized area and other related fields, fostering a holistic perspective.

2. **Communication and Collaboration:**
   - **Effective Communication:** Cultivating communication skills to convey complex ideas to individuals with diverse backgrounds.
   - **Collaborative Abilities:** Facilitating collaboration and teamwork by understanding and appreciating the contributions of colleagues from various disciplines.

3. **Problem-Solving in Different Contexts:**
   - **Adaptability:** Applying skills and problem-solving approaches to diverse situations, demonstrating adaptability.
   - **Innovation:** Leveraging the breadth of knowledge to contribute to innovative solutions that draw from various disciplines.

The Intersection-Integrating Depth and Breadth

The point where the vertical and horizontal bars intersect represents the sweet spot—the culmination of deep expertise and broad knowledge. This intersection signifies the ability to apply specialized knowledge in a cross-functional context, making individuals invaluable contributors in multidisciplinary teams.

In practical terms, individuals with T-shaped skills can excel in roles that require both specialized proficiency and collaboration across different functions. They become versatile assets, capable of driving innovation, fostering effective communication, and navigating the complexities of a rapidly evolving professional landscape. The T-shaped skills model, therefore, serves as a roadmap for well-rounded professional development, preparing individuals to thrive in diverse and dynamic work environments.

In the journey toward building a T-shaped skill set, responsibility expansion serves as a powerful catalyst for deepening expertise within a specialized domain. Individuals taking on leadership roles in specialized projects within their expanded responsibilities find opportunities to hone their specialized knowledge and skills. This may involve mentoring others, teaching, and addressing complex challenges within their well-defined area of expertise. The vertical bar of the T, representing deep proficiency, is nurtured through hands-on experience and the leadership responsibilities that come with expanded roles.

Broadening Horizons-The Cross-Functional Experience

Simultaneously, responsibility expansion contributes significantly to the horizontal bar of the T-shaped skill set—broadening knowledge across various disciplines. Involvement in cross-functional teams and leading projects that draw contributions from different departments expose individuals to diverse perspectives. Project management within this context fosters an understanding of how different functions collaborate, encouraging adaptability and a broader perspective on organizational dynamics. Navigating organizational changes or shifts in priorities becomes a learning ground for adapting to multifaceted business environments.

Integration at the Intersection-Aligning Skills for Impact

The intersection of the T-shaped skill set is where deep expertise seamlessly integrates with cross-functional versatility. Individuals align their specialized skills with organizational goals, contributing to projects that have a strategic impact. Communication skills are sharpened as responsibilities expand, enabling the effective conveyance of complex ideas to audiences from various disciplines. Leadership development in multifunctional environments becomes a natural outcome as individuals guide teams towards common goals, drawing on both their deep expertise and broad understanding.

Continuous Learning and Adaptation-The Ongoing Journey

The process of responsibility expansion ensures a continuous learning journey. Individuals actively seek diverse experiences and feedback loops as part of their expanded responsibilities. This iterative process not only refines their specialized skills but also encourages ongoing adaptation to changing demands. Embracing a mindset of continuous learning becomes a hallmark of individuals building a T-shaped skill set, contributing to their resilience and versatility in a rapidly evolving work environment.

Chapter 7

The Transition: Stepping into a Managerial Role

Being open to change is paramount in the pursuit of personal and professional growth. Embracing new responsibilities represents a gateway to unforeseen opportunities, learning experiences, and skill development. In a rapidly evolving world, where change is constant, individuals who welcome new challenges demonstrate adaptability and resilience. The ability to navigate uncharted territories not only expands one's skill set but also cultivates a mindset of continuous learning. Accepting change opens doors to innovation, fosters creativity, and positions individuals on a trajectory of constant evolution, ensuring they remain agile and well-prepared for the dynamic demands of the future.

Taking on new responsibilities is not just a task; it is an investment in personal and professional growth. New responsibilities often require individuals to step out of their comfort zones, encouraging them to develop skills that may not have been previously utilized. Whether it involves leading a project, managing a team, or tackling unfamiliar challenges, each new responsibility presents an opportunity for skill refinement and leadership development. Moreover, the successful navigation of increased responsibilities often leads to a heightened sense of accomplishment, boosting confidence and motivation for future endeavors. Each step into the unknown brings the potential for growth, paving the way for a more enriched and fulfilling professional journey.

Before boarding on the journey of new responsibilities, self-reflection becomes a crucial prerequisite for success. Understanding one's strengths, weaknesses, values, and aspirations lays the foundation for making informed decisions about the types of responsibilities to undertake. Self-reflection provides clarity on personal and professional goals, aligning new responsibilities with an individual's broader vision. It also allows for an honest assessment of the capacity to handle increased demands, ensuring that the decision to take on new responsibilities is a well-informed and mindful choice. By engaging in self-reflection, individuals can proactively identify areas for growth, set realistic expectations, and approach new responsibilities with a heightened sense of purpose and self-awareness.

Networking

Networking and learning from individuals who have successfully navigated similar transitions offer a host of invaluable benefits, constituting a powerful strategy for personal and professional growth. One of the primary advantages lies in the insights and wisdom gained from the firsthand experiences of those who have trodden similar paths. Their practical knowledge serves as a guide, offering real-world examples of challenges faced, strategies employed, and lessons learned during transitions. By tapping into this collective knowledge, individuals can gain a nuanced understanding of the transition process, ultimately shortening their learning curve.

Furthermore, connecting with individuals who have undergone similar transitions provides a crucial opportunity to avoid potential pitfalls. Learning about challenges faced by others equips individuals with a proactive mindset, enabling them to navigate their own transitions more smoothly and make informed decisions. The benefit of accelerated learning extends beyond mere avoidance of pitfalls; it encompasses a comprehensive understanding of the nuances and intricacies associated with the transition.

Networking often leads to mentorship opportunities, a pivotal aspect of professional development. Establishing connections with those who have successfully transitioned opens the door to mentor-mentee relationships. Mentors, drawing from their wealth of experience, can offer personalized guidance, share industry-specific insights, and provide invaluable advice tailored to the unique challenges of the transition. This mentorship dynamic not only accelerates learning but also offers a source of inspiration and motivation for individuals navigating similar changes.

Expanding one's professional network through connections with successful transitioners introduces individuals to new opportunities, potential collaborators, and diverse perspectives within their industry or field. This expanded network becomes a valuable resource for staying updated on industry trends, accessing job openings, and enhancing overall career prospects.

Moreover, networking with individuals who have undergone similar transitions contributes to the building of a robust support system. Transitions, by their nature, can be emotionally challenging. Sharing concerns, seeking advice, and receiving encouragement from individuals who understand the journey fosters resilience and emotional well-being. The support garnered from a like-minded network provides individuals with the confidence to face challenges head-on and navigate transitions with greater ease.

Beyond emotional support, networking facilitates access to job opportunities. Learning from others in the network can lead to insights about potential job openings, industry trends, and the hiring landscape. Recommendations and referrals from within the network enhance job prospects during a transition, showcasing the tangible benefits of a well-established professional community.

Additionally, networking exposes individuals to a diverse set of skills and competencies. Learning from others who have transitioned allows individuals to identify and develop the skills that are most relevant and valuable in their new roles or industries. This exposure to diverse skills contributes to continuous professional development and positions individuals as adaptable and versatile contributors.

Networking Strategies

1. Enrolling in Targeted Training Programs and Courses Embark on your skill development journey by enrolling in online courses and certifications offered by platforms like Coursera, Udacity, and LinkedIn Learning. These self-paced learning options provide comprehensive content and assessments tailored to specific skill sets. Additionally, consider attending professional workshops and seminars to gain hands-on insights and practical knowledge.	6. Soliciting Continuous Feedback for Iterative Learning Actively seek feedback on your progress from mentors, peers, or online communities. Constructive feedback helps identify areas for improvement and guides your ongoing learning journey. Embrace an iterative learning approach, refining your strategies based on feedback and evolving industry trends.
2. Pursuing Formal Education For a more structured approach, explore formal education options such as degree programs or advanced certifications from reputable universities and educational institutions. These programs often offer in-depth coverage of the skills you seek to acquire, providing a solid foundation through structured curricula.	7. Building a Network and Community Engagement Become part of professional associations and attend networking events to connect with industry professionals. Engage with online communities and forums related to your skills, where professionals share insights and discuss emerging trends. Networking provides valuable opportunities for learning from diverse perspectives.
3. Seeking Mentorship for Personalized Guidance The power of mentorship by identifying experienced individuals who possess the skills you aspire to develop. Cultivate mentor-mentee relationships to receive personalized guidance, industry insights, and advice. Actively participate in mentorship programs within your organization or industry for ongoing support.	8. Gaining Practical Experience through Internships and Volunteer Work Explore internships or entry-level positions to gain practical experience and exposure to real-world challenges. Additionally, consider volunteering for projects aligned with your skill development goals, combining hands-on experience with a sense of purposeful contribution.
4. Embracing Self-Directed Learning through Diverse Resources Empower yourself through self-directed learning using diverse online resources. Explore educational websites, blogs, and forums for a wealth of content. Additionally, delve into books and publications relevant to your chosen skills, allowing for deep exploration and understanding at your own pace.	9. Mastery of Technology and Tools Actively experiment with tools and technologies associated with your target skills. Hands-on experience enhances your practical proficiency. Utilize online platforms that offer virtual environments for practicing technical skills in a safe and controlled setting.
5. Engaging in Skill-Specific Workshops and Collaborative Projects Immerse yourself in hands-on learning experiences by participating in skill-specific workshops and practical training sessions. Create personal projects aligned with your skill development goals and collaborate with others on team projects. These activities provide practical application opportunities and foster a collaborative learning environment.	10. Maintaining an Iterative Approach for Skill Refinement Adopt an iterative approach to skill development, continuously refining and adapting your learning strategies. Stay informed about evolving industry trends and incorporate feedback into your skill enhancement journey. This dynamic approach ensures ongoing growth and adaptability in your skill set.

Transitioning Leadership

Transitioning from a peer to a leader introduces a set of distinct challenges and opportunities that necessitate a nuanced approach. The changed dynamics within the team requires a delicate balance between asserting authority and maintaining positive relationships. Building credibility and trust is paramount, with the need to demonstrate competence and effective decision-making. Managing conflicting loyalties between upper management and former peers demands clear communication and strategic decision alignment. Shifting from a task-oriented mindset to a strategic one underscores the challenge of focusing on broader organizational goals. Providing constructive feedback and making tough decisions become integral aspects of leadership, requiring assertiveness and a commitment to team success.

Fostering team cohesion amid the potential disruption of the transition is crucial, emphasizing the need for a positive team culture. On the flip side, transitioning offers opportunities such as leveraging unique insights into team dynamics and developing a leadership presence. Continuous learning, mentorship, and participation in leadership development programs become essential for success in the evolving leadership role.

In essence, the transition from peer to leader is a multifaceted journey that demands adaptability, self-awareness, and a proactive commitment to ongoing growth and development. Leading former peers entails steering complex psychological and interpersonal challenges that demand a high degree of emotional intelligence and self-awareness. The shift from a collaborative, peer-to-peer relationship to a leadership role can trigger feelings of resentment, skepticism, or resistance among team members who were once equals. Leaders must grapple with the psychological impact of perceived favoritism, jealousy, or doubts about their qualifications.

This dynamic creates a delicate interpersonal balance, requiring leaders to manage expectations, build trust, and address potential conflicts effectively. The importance of self-awareness in this transition cannot be overstated. Leaders must have a keen understanding of their own strengths, weaknesses, and leadership style to direct the shift authentically. Self-awareness enables leaders to proactively manage their emotions, project confidence, and adapt their leadership approach to foster a positive team dynamic.

Furthermore, empathy plays a pivotal role in understanding and validating the emotions of former peers adjusting to the new hierarchy. Leaders need to be attuned to the individual needs and concerns of team members, demonstrating a genuine understanding of their perspectives. By practicing empathy, leaders can build trust, open lines of communication, and foster a collaborative environment.

Ultimately, the successful navigation of psychological and interpersonal challenges rests on leaders' ability to cultivate self-awareness, engage in open communication, and demonstrate empathy, ensuring a smooth transition that preserves team cohesion and paves the way for effective leadership.

Leading Transformation Examples

Mary Barra's journey from an engineer to becoming the CEO of General Motors showcased her ability to lead a transformation within the company. Her emphasis on innovation, customer focus, and adaptability contributed to successfully steering the company through significant changes.

Bob Iger's leadership transition at Disney, moving from Chief Operating Officer to CEO, was marked by strategic succession planning. He demonstrated a keen understanding of Disney's culture, brand, and industry trends, ensuring a seamless transition and sustained success for the company.

Sheryl Sandberg's journey from being Facebook's Chief Operating Officer to a prominent leadership role exemplifies successful transition management. Through her tenure, she has displayed adaptability, strong interpersonal skills, and a focus on empowering her team, all critical elements in leading former peers.

Organizational Culture

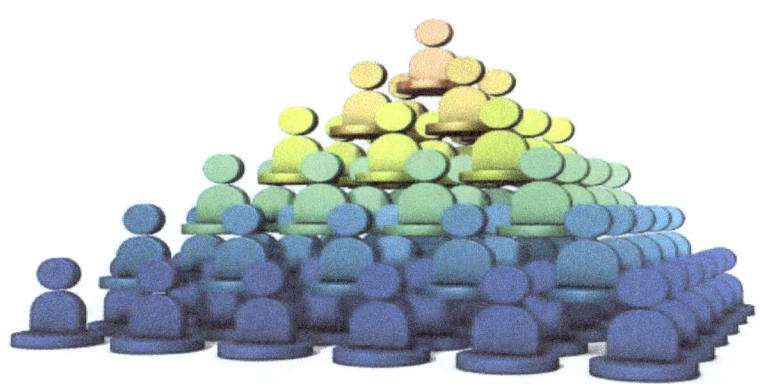

Organizational culture encompasses the shared values, beliefs, practices, and customs that define the collective identity of a company. It serves as the social fabric that shapes employee behavior, interactions, and the overall work environment. The impact of organizational culture on leadership is multifaceted, influencing leadership styles, decision-making processes, and the overall dynamics within the organization.

Leadership styles are often influenced by the prevailing organizational culture. In a culture that values innovation and risk-taking, leaders may adopt transformational or entrepreneurial leadership styles, encouraging creativity and experimentation. Conversely, in a more traditional or risk-averse culture, leaders may lean towards a more transactional or bureaucratic leadership approach, emphasizing stability and adherence to established processes.

Organizational culture significantly impacts employee engagement and motivation. A positive and inclusive culture that values employee well-being, personal growth, and collaboration can enhance leadership effectiveness. Leaders who understand and leverage the positive aspects of the culture can create work environments where employees feel inspired, motivated, and connected to the organization's mission.

The decision-making processes within an organization are often influenced by its culture. In a culture that values consensus and collaboration, leaders may adopt participative decision-making approaches, seeking input from team members. In contrast, in a culture that emphasizes efficiency and hierarchy, leaders may make more autocratic decisions. Effective leaders recognize and adapt their decision-making and communication styles to align with the cultural context, promoting understanding and acceptance among team members.

Leaders play a pivotal role in shaping and, if necessary, transforming organizational culture. When faced with the need for cultural change, leaders act as change agents by embodying the desired values, fostering open communication, and aligning organizational practices with the intended cultural shift. This process requires leadership commitment, consistency, and the ability to navigate resistance, ultimately influencing the collective mindset of the workforce.

Organizational culture sets the tone for employee behavior and performance expectations. Leaders, as cultural stewards, guide and reinforce expected behaviors through their own actions and decisions. A culture that encourages innovation and collaboration tends to result in higher levels of employee engagement and performance. Leaders who actively promote and model these cultural attributes contribute to a positive work environment and improved organizational outcomes.

Organizational culture also influences an organization's adaptability and resilience. In rapidly changing environments, a culture that embraces learning, flexibility, and innovation supports effective leadership in navigating challenges. Leaders who understand the cultural context can foster adaptability by encouraging a growth mindset and the ability to embrace change as a collective effort.

Leadership development programs often incorporate cultural assessments to help leaders understand and navigate the cultural dynamics of their organizations. These assessments provide insights into the existing culture, enabling leaders to tailor their approaches and strategies for maximum effectiveness.

Aligning Leadership Style

Cultural Cohesion: Aligning one's leadership style with the values and norms of the organization is paramount for fostering cultural cohesion. When a leader's approach resonates with the established cultural elements, it creates a shared sense of purpose and identity within the team. Team members are more likely to collaborate effectively when they perceive a congruence between their leader's style and the organization's values. This alignment minimizes conflicts arising from differing values, ensuring a unified and harmonious workplace culture.

Employee Engagement: Leaders who align their leadership style with organizational values contribute significantly to employee engagement. When employees observe that their leader embodies and promotes the same values, it establishes a connection between the leader and the organizational culture. This connection enhances job satisfaction, commitment, and a sense of belonging among team members. Engaged employees are more likely to be motivated, productive, and less prone to turnover, resulting in a positive impact on overall organizational performance.

Trust and Credibility: Alignment between leadership style and organizational values is fundamental for building trust and credibility. Consistency in demonstrating behaviors that align with organizational values fosters trust among team members. When leaders adhere to the established values, employees are more likely to trust their decisions and guidance. This trust is a cornerstone of effective leadership, contributing to open communication, transparency, and a positive organizational climate.

Cultural Reinforcement: Leaders serve as key influencers within an organization, and their alignment with organizational values reinforces those values throughout the workforce. By consistently embodying and promoting the established values, leaders contribute to cultural reinforcement. This process helps solidify the desired cultural norms, sending a clear message to employees about the organization's commitment to its guiding principles. The continuous reinforcement of values ensures that the cultural fabric remains intact and resilient.

Adaptability and Change Management: Leadership alignment with organizational values becomes particularly critical during periods of change. When leaders adhere to the established values, employees are more likely to embrace and adapt to changes seamlessly. The consistency in values provides a stable foundation during times of uncertainty, helping organizations navigate transitions with minimal resistance. This alignment fosters a culture of adaptability, where employees are more receptive to change initiatives, ultimately contributing to the organization's long-term success.

Decision-Making Consistency: Alignment between leadership style and organizational values ensures consistency in decision-making processes. When leaders make decisions that reflect the organization's values, it promotes fairness and equity. Consistent decision-making contributes to a sense of justice among employees, reinforcing the organization's commitment to its guiding principles. This consistency enhances the predictability of leadership actions and fosters a positive perception of organizational governance.

Organizational Reputation: Leaders who align their leadership style with organizational values contribute to the positive reputation of the organization. External stakeholders, including customers, partners, and the broader community, perceive the organization as principled and ethical. This positive reputation enhances the organization's attractiveness and competitiveness in the market. A strong alignment between leadership and organizational values becomes a valuable asset in building a reputable brand image.

Long-Term Organizational Success: Leadership styles that align with organizational values are integral to the long-term success and sustainability of the organization. A shared commitment to values provides a stable foundation for growth, innovation, and resilience. It helps create an organizational identity that resonates with employees, customers, and stakeholders, fostering loyalty and longevity. The alignment between leadership and organizational values is a strategic investment in the enduring success of the organization.

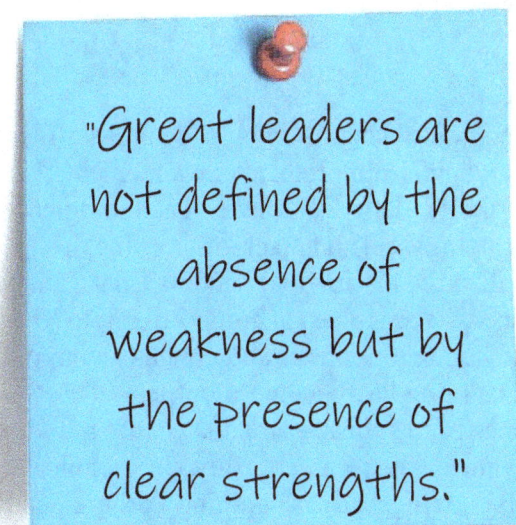

"Great leaders are not defined by the absence of weakness but by the presence of clear strengths."

Chapter **8**

Thriving as a New Manager

The contemporary land of knowledge and skills is undergoing a profound evolution, primarily driven by rapid technological advancements, global interconnectedness, and the dynamic nature of the modern workplace. Technological progress, notably in areas like automation, artificial intelligence, and machine learning, has reshaped industries and given rise to a demand for specialized skills in fields such as data analytics, coding, and cybersecurity. This tech-centric shift necessitates a commitment to continuous learning as the digital revolution transforms job requirements and creates an ongoing demand for updated competencies.

Lifelong learning has become a cornerstone of personal and professional development. The pace of change in industries mandates that individuals adopt a mindset of perpetual learning to stay relevant in their careers. Beyond technical expertise, the importance of soft skills and emotional intelligence is gaining prominence. Effective communication, adaptability, collaboration, and empathy are recognized as essential attributes in workplaces where teamwork, creativity, and human interaction play pivotal roles.

The merging of traditional disciplines is a notable trend, with problem-solving increasingly requiring an interdisciplinary approach. Professionals equipped with diverse skill sets spanning technology, business, and social sciences are better positioned to address the multifaceted challenges of today's complex environment. Globalization has heightened the importance of cultural competence and international perspectives. Individuals who can navigate and collaborate in diverse cultural settings are increasingly valued in an era where businesses operate on a global scale.

Creativity and innovation have become critical components of success in the knowledge economy. Organizations prioritize individuals who can think creatively, generate innovative ideas, and contribute to problem-solving in novel ways. Alongside this, the focus on environmental sustainability and social responsibility has led to a demand for skills related to sustainable practices, corporate social responsibility, and ethical decision-making.

Critical thinking and analytical skills are essential in an information-saturated world. The ability to evaluate and analyze data critically, coupled with evidence-based decision-making, is crucial for navigating the complexities of contemporary issues. Additionally, the rise of remote work and digital collaboration tools has transformed the nature of teamwork. Skills related to effective communication in virtual environments, online collaboration, and digital project management have become integral for professionals working in distributed and global teams.

The vitality of adaptability and continuous learning in staying relevant cannot be excessive in the evolving business world.

1. Technological Advancements

The ever-accelerating pace of technological innovation means that skills and knowledge can quickly become obsolete. Adaptability is crucial for individuals to direct the changing technological landscape. Continuous learning allows professionals to stay abreast of emerging technologies, acquire new skills, and ensure their expertise remains relevant in an increasingly digital world.

2. Industry Evolution

Industries are undergoing transformative changes driven by factors such as automation, artificial intelligence, and changing consumer behaviors. Professionals who adapt and engage in continuous learning are better positioned to understand industry trends, anticipate shifts, and proactively align their skills with the evolving needs of their respective sectors.

3. Globalization and Diverse Environments

Globalization has interconnected economies and created a more diverse and interconnected workforce. Adaptability is crucial for navigating diverse cultural settings, different working norms, and global collaboration. Continuous learning fosters cross-cultural competency, enabling individuals to effectively engage with international counterparts and thrive in a globally integrated environment.

4. Career Resilience

In a world where job roles and career paths are constantly evolving, adaptability and continuous learning contribute to career resilience. Professionals who actively seek new knowledge and skills are better equipped to pivot in their careers, explore new opportunities, and weather industry disruptions. This resilience is a key factor in staying relevant and sustaining long-term employability.

5. Innovation and Problem-Solving

Adaptability and continuous learning fuel innovation and problem-solving. Individuals who embrace a mindset of continual improvement are more likely to approach challenges with creativity and find innovative solutions. The ability to adapt to new information and leverage diverse knowledge sets enhances problem-solving capabilities, fostering a culture of innovation in both individual and organizational contexts.

6. Changing Work Environments

The nature of work is evolving, with an increasing emphasis on remote work, flexible schedules, and collaborative digital platforms. Professionals need to adapt to new work environments, leveraging technology for effective communication and collaboration. Continuous learning ensures individuals stay proficient in the use of digital tools and navigate the evolving dynamics of contemporary workplaces.

7. Future-Proofing Skills

Adaptability and continuous learning serve as a form of future-proofing skills. As industries undergo transformation and new roles emerge, individuals who are adaptable and committed to learning are better positioned to acquire the skills demanded by the future job market. This proactive approach mitigates the risk of skill obsolescence and enhances long-term career prospects.

Stories of Successful Individuals

Elon Musk, the visionary entrepreneur behind companies like Tesla and SpaceX, exemplifies a relentless learning mindset. Despite not having a traditional background in rocket science, Musk taught himself the principles of aerospace engineering and successfully founded SpaceX. His ability to immerse himself in diverse fields, from electric vehicles to renewable energy, showcases a continuous thirst for knowledge and a commitment to pushing the boundaries of innovation.

Sal Khan, the founder of Khan Academy, is a former hedge fund analyst who transformed into an educator and entrepreneur. Recognizing the need for accessible education, Khan started creating online tutorials to help his cousin with math. This evolved into Khan Academy, a non-profit offering free online education. Khan's story highlights how a passion for learning and a commitment to making education accessible can lead to groundbreaking initiatives.

Temie Giwa-Tubosun is the founder of LifeBank, a Nigerian health tech startup. Initially trained as a biochemist, she pursued a career in global health and technology. Giwa-Tubosun's commitment to addressing blood shortages in Nigeria through innovative solutions showcases her adaptability and a learning mindset. She constantly seeks new ways to leverage technology to improve healthcare delivery in resource-constrained   settings.

Angela Duckworth, a psychologist and author of "Grit," is known for her work on the importance of passion and perseverance. Despite initially pursuing a career in consulting, Duckworth shifted her focus to psychology, eventually earning a Ph.D. from the University of Pennsylvania. Her dedication to understanding grit and the psychology of achievement reflects a commitment to lifelong learning and adapting one's path in pursuit of a greater understanding of human behavior.

Satya Nadella, the CEO of Microsoft, is recognized for his transformative leadership. When Nadella took over the reins, he emphasized a cultural shift toward empathy and a growth mindset within the company. His own journey from an electrical engineering background to becoming a leader in the tech industry reflects a commitment to continuous learning and adaptation. Nadella's leadership style highlights the importance of fostering a learning culture within organizations.

Impact of Mentors

The impact of mentors and a strong support network on professional development is multifaceted and pivotal in shaping the trajectory of individuals' careers. Mentors serve as guides and sources of wisdom, facilitating the transfer of knowledge and skills gained through their own experiences. This mentorship dynamic accelerates the professional growth of mentees by providing insights into industry-specific nuances, offering practical advice, and helping navigate the complexities of the professional landscape. Furthermore, mentors play a crucial role in career guidance, assisting mentees in setting and achieving their professional goals. Through sharing personal journeys, mentors inspire and empower their mentees to overcome challenges and strive for success.

A strong support network, which often includes mentors, extends beyond one-on-one relationships to encompass a broader community. This network creates a rich tapestry of connections, opening doors to valuable networking opportunities and fostering collaborative environments. Mentors introduce their mentees to industry professionals, creating a bridge to new relationships and enhancing visibility within the professional community. The diversity of thought within this network contributes to a dynamic ecosystem where individuals gain exposure to varied perspectives, enhancing critical thinking and adaptability.

Emotional support is a cornerstone of the mentor-mentee relationship and a strong support network. The highs and lows of a career can be emotionally taxing, and having mentors and a community to share successes, setbacks, and concerns with provides a valuable outlet. This emotional support bolsters confidence, resilience, and a sense of belonging within the professional community.

The impact of mentors and a robust support network also extends to accelerating the learning curve of individuals. Mentors share their experiences, lessons learned from successes and failures, and practical insights, allowing mentees to benefit from an expedited learning process. Leveraging the collective knowledge within a support network enhances professionals' ability to stay informed about industry trends, technological advancements, and emerging opportunities, fostering a culture of continuous learning and adaptability.

Additionally, mentors often act as advocates for their mentees, promoting their talents and contributions within professional circles. This advocacy can lead to increased visibility, career advancement opportunities, and a positive reputation within the industry. A strong support network further contributes to a culture where individuals champion each other's success, creating a collaborative and mutually beneficial professional environment.

Formal Mentorship

1. Organizational Mentorship Programs

Many organizations institute formal mentorship programs to pair experienced employees with those seeking guidance. These structured initiatives often involve goal setting, regular meetings, and predefined learning objectives. Organizational mentorship programs provide a framework for mentees to navigate their careers with the support of seasoned mentors.

2. Professional Associations and Networks

Professional associations frequently facilitate formal mentorship programs to connect members within a specific industry or field. These programs offer a structured approach to mentorship, fostering relationships that extend beyond the workplace and providing mentees with access to a broader professional community.

3. Academic Mentorship Programs

Within educational institutions, formal mentorship programs connect students with faculty or industry professionals. These programs aim to guide students through academic challenges, career choices, and research opportunities. Academic mentorship often follows a structured curriculum and involves regular check-ins to assess progress.

Informal Mentorship

1. Peer Mentorship

Peer mentorship is an informal arrangement where individuals at similar career stages support each other. Colleagues or friends within the same organization or industry provide guidance, share experiences, and offer advice on navigating shared professional challenges. Peer mentorship often evolves organically and is based on mutual trust and camaraderie.

2. Reverse Mentorship

Reverse mentorship involves a less experienced individual providing insights and guidance to a more seasoned professional, often in areas such as technology, social trends, or emerging industry practices. This form of mentorship fosters a culture of mutual learning and knowledge exchange.

3. Virtual Mentorship

In today's digital age, mentorship can take place virtually, transcending geographical boundaries. Virtual mentorship often occurs through video calls, email exchanges, or online platforms. This flexible arrangement enables mentees to connect with mentors outside their immediate physical proximity, expanding the pool of potential mentors.

4. Situational Mentorship

Informal mentorship can also be situational, arising in response to specific challenges or projects. Individuals seek guidance from colleagues or mentors who possess expertise in a particular area, forming temporary mentorship arrangements to address immediate needs.

5. Community-based Mentorship

Mentorship can extend beyond the workplace to community-based programs. Professionals may engage in informal mentorship within community organizations, non-profits, or volunteer initiatives. This form of mentorship contributes to personal development while fostering a sense of social responsibility.

6. Self-directed Mentorship

Some individuals take a proactive approach to mentorship by seeking out role models, industry influencers, or thought leaders. This self-directed mentorship involves learning from others through various mediums such as books, podcasts, and online content.

The Concept of Fairness

Fairness is a fundamental principle that underpins effective leadership. In the context of leadership, fairness refers to the equitable and just treatment of individuals, irrespective of their background, characteristics, or position within an organization. Fairness is crucial for building trust, fostering a positive organizational culture, and promoting employee engagement. Leaders who prioritize fairness create an inclusive environment where individuals feel valued and respected, ultimately contributing to a motivated and productive workforce.

Fairness in leadership involves several key elements:

- **Equitable Treatment:** Leaders should ensure that individuals are treated fairly and without discrimination. This extends to opportunities for professional growth, recognition, and the allocation of resources.
- **Consistency:** Fair leaders apply consistent standards and rules to all individuals. Consistency in decision-making fosters a sense of predictability and trust within the organization.
- Open Communication: Fairness also involves transparent and open communication. Leaders should communicate decisions clearly, providing rationale and context to help individuals understand the reasoning behind various actions.

The Significance of Fairness, Accountability, and Transparency in Leadership Roles

Fairness is closely intertwined with accountability and transparency in leadership. These principles form the bedrock of ethical leadership and contribute to the establishment of a positive organizational climate.

- **Accountability:** Leaders must be accountable for their decisions and actions. This involves taking responsibility for outcomes, acknowledging mistakes, and actively seeking solutions to rectify any shortcomings. When leaders demonstrate accountability, they set a precedent for the entire organization to take responsibility for their contributions.
- **Transparency:** Transparent leadership involves openness in decision-making processes and sharing relevant information with stakeholders. Transparent leaders provide visibility into the rationale behind decisions, organizational goals, and performance metrics. This transparency builds trust and fosters a culture of honesty within the workplace.

The Role of Impartiality, Equity, and Justice in Decision-Making

Impartiality, equity, and justice are integral components of fair decision-making in leadership.

- **Impartiality:** Leaders must approach decision-making without bias or favoritism. Impartial leaders consider all relevant factors objectively, ensuring that decisions are based on merit rather than personal preferences. This approach promotes a sense of fairness and integrity within the organization.
- **Equity:** Equity involves recognizing and addressing individual needs and differences to ensure that everyone has an equal opportunity to succeed. Leaders should strive for equity in resource distribution, professional development opportunities, and recognition. This commitment to equity contributes to a diverse and inclusive workplace.
- **Justice:** Just leaders prioritize fairness and ensure that individuals are treated ethically and in accordance with established standards. Justice in leadership involves upholding ethical principles, adhering to legal standards, and promoting a sense of fairness in all interactions.

Chapter **9**

Case Study

Case Study By: https://hbr.org/2012/04/the-real-leadership-lessons-of-steve-jobs

Do We Underestimate the Importance of Leadership?

Steve Jobs' entrepreneurial journey is akin to the creation myths of business legends. Co-founding Apple in his parents' garage in 1976, facing ousting in 1985, and returning to rescue the company from near bankruptcy in 1997, Jobs transformed it into the world's most valuable company by his death in 2011. His impact reached across seven industries, including personal computing, animated movies, music, phones, tablet computing, retail stores, and digital publishing. In the league of great American innovators like Edison, Ford, and Disney, Jobs' legacy lies in applying imagination to technology and business.

Despite not being a saint, his personality was a crucial aspect of his business approach. Acting as if normal rules didn't apply, Jobs infused passion, intensity, and extreme emotionalism into both his personal life and the products he created. His perfectionism, coupled with petulance and impatience, shaped his leadership style. Reflecting on his tendency to be demanding, Jobs pointed to the results and the loyalty of his smart and capable team.

The accomplishments over the years, including the iMac, iPod, iPhone, and numerous other hits, surpassed those of any other innovative company in modern times. As he battled his final illness, Jobs was surrounded by a loyal group of colleagues and a supportive family. The true lessons from Steve Jobs lie in examining his achievements. According to Jobs, his most important creation was not a specific product like the iPad or Macintosh but Apple the company.

Making an enduring company, he believed, was more challenging and significant than creating a great product. The keys to his success, which business schools may study for centuries, include his ability to think differently, his dedication to making an enduring company, and the impact of his intense personality on innovation and achievement.

Upon Steve Jobs' return to Apple in 1997, he confronted a chaotic product lineup, featuring a multitude of computers and peripherals, causing confusion and inefficiency. Jobs, known for his focus, took immediate action. He gathered his team, grabbed a Magic Marker, and drew a two-by-two grid on a whiteboard. Labeling the columns "Consumer" and "Pro" and the rows "Desktop" and "Portable," he directed the team to concentrate on four great products, one for each quadrant, and eliminate all others. This move, driven by Jobs' belief that deciding what not to do is as crucial as deciding what to do, ultimately saved the company.

Jobs continued to emphasize focus by annually taking his top 100 people on retreats. During these sessions, he would challenge them to identify the ten most important initiatives for the company. However, Jobs, ever the advocate for simplicity, would cross off suggestions he deemed unwise and limit the final list to only three priorities. This rigorous prioritization mirrored his Zen training, filtering out distractions and maintaining laser-like focus on essential tasks.

Simplicity, another hallmark of Jobs' approach, was rooted in his Zen-like ability to concentrate on the essence of things. His quest for simplicity was evident in Apple's design philosophy, epitomized by the slogan, "Simplicity is the ultimate sophistication." Jobs admired Atari's simplicity during his early career and sought to emulate it in Apple's products. When presented with Xerox's complex computer design, he simplified it, creating a more intuitive interface. Jobs believed in conquering complexity to achieve a friendly user experience.

Collaborating with Jony Ive, Apple's industrial designer, Jobs aimed for deep simplicity that went beyond mere aesthetics. To eliminate unnecessary components, they delved into the fundamental purpose of each element. This approach required a profound understanding of challenges and the development of elegant solutions. For instance, in designing the iPod interface, Jobs insisted on reducing clutter, aiming for accessibility within three clicks.

Jobs' pursuit of simplicity extended beyond products to disrupt industries that unnecessarily complicated user experiences. The iPod and iTunes Store targeted convoluted music players and online song acquisition, while his dissatisfaction with the complexity of mobile phones inspired the creation of the iPhone. Even in his final years, Jobs turned his attention to simplifying the television industry, reflecting his enduring commitment to making technology more accessible and user-friendly.

Achieving simplicity, according to Jobs, involved seamless integration of hardware, software, and peripheral devices within the Apple ecosystem. Taking end-to-end responsibility for the user experience set Apple apart, contrasting with more open approaches by companies like **Microsoft and Google.**

Jobs' compulsion to control every aspect of the user experience stemmed from his personality and passion for perfection. This approach, though not always maximizing short-term profits, led to astonishing products and delightful user experiences, akin to walking in a Zen garden.

Innovation for Jobs meant not only coming up with new ideas but also leapfrogging when behind. The creation of the iPod and iTunes, for example, was a response to the iMac's initial deficiency in dealing with music, showcasing Jobs' ability to stay ahead.

Putting products before profits was a key philosophy. Jobs believed in focusing on creating great products, trusting that profits would follow. This stood in contrast to profit-driven approaches that often led to a decline in product quality.

Rejecting the reliance on focus groups, Jobs emphasized deep empathy and intuition for understanding customer desires. Rather than asking customers what they wanted, he aimed to create products that they would love, using his and his friends' preferences as a guide.

Jobs' Reality Distortion Field, though seen as demanding, pushed his team to achieve the impossible. It was a driving force that led to extraordinary feats and breakthroughs in the face of seemingly insurmountable challenges.

Imputing importance to presentation and packaging, Jobs understood the impact of the first impression. He meticulously designed not only the visible parts of Apple products but also the packaging, considering the unveiling experience as a crucial aspect of product perception.

Jobs' pursuit of perfection extended to pausing development when he felt a product wasn't just right. This perfectionism applied to both visible and invisible elements, from the external design to the internal circuit boards of Apple devices.

Tolerating only "A" players, Jobs' tough management style aimed to prevent mediocrity and maintain a team of high performers. Despite his rough approach, he instilled passion and loyalty in his team, creating a close-knit Apple family.

Emphasizing face-to-face meetings, Jobs valued spontaneous interactions and believed in the creativity that arises from unplanned encounters. This was reflected in the design of Apple's offices, fostering collaboration and innovation.

Jobs' ability to see both the big picture and the smallest details set him apart. From grand visions like the digital hub concept to concerns about the color of screws, he combined strategic thinking with a focus on design minutiae.

Combining the humanities with the sciences was a central theme in Jobs' life. He saw the intersection of creativity and technology as the key to innovation. Jobs' ability to merge poetry with processors defined his approach to building groundbreaking products.

Jobs' final message, "Stay Hungry, Stay Foolish," encapsulated his lifelong philosophy influenced by both the counterculture and the tech culture. It reflected his perpetual hunger for innovation and his willingness to embrace a certain level of foolishness in the pursuit of groundbreaking ideas.

Chapter **10**

Building a Visionary Mindset an Introduction

Welcome to "Leader's Anchor Ship Chapter 10"! In this exciting chapter, we will dive into the fascinating world of building a visionary mindset. If you want to activate your creativity and be inspired by profound words that will challenge and change you, this is the chapter for you. Whether an up-and-coming entrepreneur seeking success or someone who just wants to be innovative in business life: Wisdom-Focused Leader provides insight and strategy on how to navigate these treacherous waters towards victory against all odds!

Building a visionary mindset is essential in today's high-speed, constantly changing environment. It lets people break out of the mold, question norms and stretch

to what is imaginable or desirable. A visionary mindset enables businesses to predict trends, forecast innovative products and provide leadership with assurance. The visionary mindset has spoken about its capacity to foresee trends predictively, create ground-breaking solutions, and lead with confidence.

In this chapter, we'll explore what components you need to install in yourself – to make it possible for a person like you who isn't particularly open to change to do so. We will delve into the power of visionary thinking, the importance of embracing change, fostering creativity and innovation, setting inspiring goals, and much more. Whether you're an old hand in the business world wanting to enhance your leadership skills, or just an individual seeking self-improvement and greater returns in life– all this knowledge will provide a firm foundation for building your visionary mindset.

So fasten your seat belts tightly! We're off on a journey of transformation. Let's go forth towards the construction of a visionary mindset leading to success, innovation, and a wealth of possibilities.

Understanding Visionary Thinking

In order to instill a visionary mindset, it is important first to understand visionary thinking. Visionary thinking goes beyond conventional ideas; it spurs creativity and forward-thinking thoughts. It requires not only the ability toa analyze situations from different points of view but also foresee future trends and create innovative solutions.

In today's fast-changing world, thinking like a visionary is just what we need to get ahead of the curve and cope with the pressures of a transition phase. If you start to think in these terms, open yourself up to that kind of visionary thinking, you will develop a mind which is curious and enthusiastic about novelty, and ready to challenge accepted Received Wisdom.

Fostering a Growth Mindset

A visionary outlook on the world simply cannot be achieved without a growth mindset. When facing challenges, gaining insight from failure and fostering an attitude of continuous development etc. in this way Growing out of a growth mindset is an art.

People who have a growth mindset understand that their talents and intelligence can be developed with passion and effort. A growth mindset makes it easier for individuals to stretch themselves beyond their comfort zones in order to take on new challenges and confront the unknown.

Learning from failure is another important aspect of a growth mindset. People who think this way don't view their mistakes as failures, but regard them as precious opportunities for learning. They become aware of their mistakes and extract useful lessons from them to apply to future endeavors. If people with a growth mindset build failure into the process of success along the way, they can recover more quickly from setbacks and ultimately become more tenacious.

Effort is the best way to nurture a growth mindset. People should maintain an understanding of how important their own hard work and devotion are for success as well as for growth. This means that one must always strive to learn—to continue.\nWe need to know this in both our personal and work lives for self-improvement and growth.

The Benefits of a Growth Mindset:

Overcoming challenges and looking at them as opportunities to grow

Learning from your mistakes and using them as stepping stones to success

Understanding how much effort and dedication it represents to achieve any progress in personal development or professional growth.

Maintain an Openness to New Experiences and Continuous Growth.

Letting setbacks develop resilience, and bounce back stronger afterwards

Developing a growth mindset is an ongoing process, requiring regular self-examination, determination, and a readiness to break through one's own limits. It is this sort of mindset that generates creativity and innovation, and thus what gives rise to a visionary attitude.

Stimulating Creativity and Innovation

To possess such a mindset, creativity and innovation are indispensable. By unearthing our creative potential and creating an environment IDEAL for innovation, we can come up with not only new ideas but also ways of thinking that break the mold.

Below are ways to encourage creativity and innovation:

Embrace Curiosity: Keep asking questions and try to gain new perspectives on everything, Don't just ACCEPT anything as given. Curiosity, in short, is a primary force behind creativity. It's also the bridge to new ideas.

Encourage Diverse Perspectives: Set up an atmosphere that recognizes diversity and allows people to bring their unique perspectives. Then by joining together people with many different backgrounds, experiences, and skills,you can pool innumerably novel approaches to problems. Provide Time for Exploration: Set aside a specific time for experiments and new attempts. Encourage employees to become involved in personal projects, combine departments for more holistic work, or try different methods.

Develop a Growth Mindset: So the team can excel under pressure, let the members grow up with a mentality conducive to growth. Go out on a limb but support them if what they are trying fails. This kind of thinking builds a capacity for enduring setbacks and the power to keep innovating.

Create a Supportive Environment: Go ahead and promote a creative environment, a place and atmosphere conducive for taking risks. Here people are encouraged to speak freely, and ideas are always appreciated. Accept criticism and strive for personal improvement.

By implementing these strategies, organizations and individuals can build a culture of creativity and innovation, which gives them a creative way of thinking that will result in problem solving. To become even more embraced with an open attitude of constantly changing environments.

Embracing Change in a World of Uncertainty

To develop a visionary mindset, one must be able to cope with change and uncertainty. In this fast-paced world, adaptability is the key to keeping ahead. By accepting and even welcoming change, we open ourselves up to new possibilities and potential for growth.

Embracing uncertainty is a challenge, but it's also a chance to innovate and traverse undisciplined territory. In uncertainty there is the opportunity to turn our backs on old rules and strike out for new ground.

Adaptability is a powerful quality that makes it possible for us to cope with unexpected challenges. It helps us to respond quickly and gracefully to unknown situations. By cultivating adaptability, we can thrive in an ever-changing world.

To embrace change and uncertainty, consider the following strategies:

1. **Foster a Growth Mindset: See challenges as opportunities for growth and learning.**
   Embrace failures as learning experiences that can lead to improvement.
   View feedback (mistakes) as constructive suggestions for your personal and professional development.
2. **Stay Curious and Open-Minded**
   Embrace a mindset of lifelong learning and exploration.

Seek out different perspectives and ideas.

Be prepared to adapt as the world changes around you.

3. **Build Resilience**
   Develop your coping mechanisms to help you be able to handle the stress of adversity.

Build a support network of trusted mentors and peers.

Practice self-care to keep yourself physically healthy and mentally at ease.

We can unlock our full potential as visionaries by embracing change and uncertainty. They are opportunities to innovate and change in such times of uncertainty. It is during these times of uncertainty and change that we innovate, grow, and succeed.

Setting Bold and Inspiring Goals

One of the preconditions for developing a visionary mentality is the setting of demanding and inspiring objectives. While these goals urge us to surpass our own limits, they also spur our drive for innovation and enterprise.

In order to achieve bold and inspiring goals, here are a few other important strategies:

Think big: Don't set your sights too low. Instead, you should be constantly ambitious and always set yourself goals which go beyond your present abilities or current reality in society.

Define your purpose: what is your purpose in setting these goals? Your goals become more inspiring and meaningful when they are combined with some greater purpose or vision.

Break it down: Divide your great goals into smaller, bite-sized portions that are easy to tackle one at a time. In this way they will be seen to be less overwhelming as well as easier to monitor progress on from beginning to end.

Embrace discomfort: Bold goals often involve stepping outside of your comfort zone. Embrace discomfort and take risks as you pursue your vision.

Stay committed: A visionary mindset requires long-term commitment. Remain dedicated to your goals and stay focused, even when faced with trouble and disappointment.

By setting bold and inspiring goals, you create a roadmap for growth and innovation. As you live out your vision and act upon it, these aims have the power not only to change your own life but to change things on a global scale.

Cultivating a Learning Culture

The key to developing a visionary mindset is to build a learning culture. Continuing to learn, be willing to receive feedback and remaining curious - these are the crucial elements that create an atmosphere of growth and innovation.

Here are some important strategies to cultivate a learning culture:

Develop a thirst for knowledge: Create a work environment where employees are motivated to enrich themselves by studying in their spare time or taking classes. But it can be supportive if you provide for books, Internet offerings or cultural activities--these are also means to learning.

Offer the chance for employees to study comfortably. Know something new; Attend regular training soirees, seminars, and conferences on new ideas as well as industry trends. Have them disseminated among peers.

View failure as an opportunity to learn: The spirit of failed attempts should be one sees them as learning experiences, not literal setbacks. It is an environment where people can take risks, make mistakes and learn from them.

Provide feedback and recognition: Use regular critiques to improve one's skills and performance. Employees who seek after the knowledge and bring it to work should be acknowledged and rewarded.

Promote collaboration and knowledge sharing: Let employees join hands in sharing what they know. Design opportunities for interdisciplinary projects, and foster mentoring relationships.

By cultivating a learning culture, organizations can create an environment that values growth and creativity and stimulates people to constantly improve and adapt. A learning culture is the cornerstone of having a visionary mindset that promotes personal and professional success.

Builda a Diverse and Cooperative Leadership Team

A diverse and cooperative team which can forge cohesive groups in order to build a bright future. So in forming a diverse and collaborative team, one should encourage different perspectives, backgrounds, and skills.

The team members can be of different races, sexes, ages and cultural backgrounds. When diverse people work together, they bring all sorts of different views to their problems. This diversity of opinion fosters greater creativity and helps teams avoid the hazards of Groupthink. Collaboration is also important. When the members of different work teams come together, they often benefit from each other's strengths and skills. This leads to more complete solutions with greater impact and effectiveness than those produced in isolation. In addition, collaboration through parallel processes results in mutual exchange of information that can lead to breakthroughs.

An organization promoting a diverse and collaborative team can derive numerous benefits. For instance better decision-making, greater ease with change, increased problem-solving capability, and more creativity. In addition, a diverse and collective team fosters a culture of inclusiveness where everyone within the tribe is esteemed and empowered.

Diverse teams are able to provide a wider range of viewpoints and ideas

Working together with a diverse and collaborative group boosts productivity and output.

In general, building a diverse and collaborative team is a necessary aspect of visionary thinking. Such a team allows an organization to utilize the power of varied viewpoints and skills. This can lead to greater success in innovation, business growth and the good life for all.

Maintain a Vision for the Future

A visionary mindset cannot be achieved all at once; it requires constant effort and dedication. For a visionary mindset, it is essential to focus on personal growth. This process includes facing new challenges and finding ways to learn or improve oneself.

Moreover, maintaining a visionary mindset through self-care is important. Keeping the body and mind in working order maintains the necessary energy and focus for creative thinking or problem solving. Now, whether it is through exercise, meditation, or participating in various activities that catch your interest, investing some effort in looking after yourself is an investment in maintaining a visionary mindset.

Besides, to uphold a visionary mind, adapting and being changed is the true thing. With the world changing so fast, these who want it are looking at change as an opportunity. By staying open to new ideas, technologies, and perspectives.

Chapter 11

Leadership during Change and Transformation

Welcome to Chapter 11 of Leader's Anchor Ship. In this chapter, we will discuss the important subject of leading through change and transformation. As a leader, you must have specific strategies for guiding your teams successfully through periods of change and instilling confidence in your team members.

In today's dynamic business landscape, change is inevitable; thus, it is fundamental for leaders to develop the necessary skills and mindsets in order to navigate these transformations effectively. This chapter will look at strategies for leading teams through transient periods, building resilience and effective communication. In addition, we shall dig into how personal transformational leaderships by example can inspire positive changes in an organization.

Most times when change happen people tend to resist but there will be shown ways to overcome such resistance leading to successful implementation. Throughout the transformation journey, empowering and engaging your teams will be very important therefore we shall look into employee involvement enhancing strategies that can foster ownership. Furthermore we are going to review what essential skills and competencies required in effective management of change and transformational leadership.

Times of transition always come with uncertainty hence leaders are faced with the challenge of navigating it through ambiguity. Finally, this chapter will help you to thrive amidst uncertainty as well as make informed decisions that drive successful transformations happening around you. Lastly, sustaining change and ensuring long-term success and adaptability will be explored within the scope of embedding change in the culture of your company.

Please join us on an enlightening experience where you will learn how to lead through process changes using various tools available now-a-days". This paper uncovers ideas regarding guiding teams during times of changes by developing confidence among them where opportunities lie". Henceforth together we shall discover our potentiality as leaders while steering our organizations towards a secure future".

Embracing Change: The Key To Successful Transformation

For organizations seeking successful transformation in today's fast-paced business world embracing change is a way forward. Leaders must go beyond adaptation to embrace change, creating a culture of innovation and agility. Through embracing change, leaders can drive successful transformation initiatives and propel their organizations towards a brighter future.

Embracing change calls for a paradigm shift which sees it as an opportunity rather than a threat to exploitation. It also involves encouraging experimentation and calculated risk taking among employees that will help them come up with innovative ideas for addressing business challenges. In so doing, leaders who embrace change can tap into the collective wisdom of their teams thus initiating numerous innovative possibilities.

Leaders must be open-minded enough to challenge the status quo if they want to effectively embrace change. A leader's role is to inspire and motivate their followers while providing purpose and vision which are aligned with the organization's transformational goals. By communicating reasons for the desired changes as well as possible benefits, trust will be built among members thereby engaging workers in accepting such changes.

Below are key aspects of embracing change that contribute to successful transformation:

Mindset Shift: Changing your mindset from fixed to growth mentality where opportunities arise instead of threats.

Culture of Innovation: Creating an environment that fosters experimentation, creativity and generation of new ideas.

Empowered Teams: Allowing staff members to take charge and contribute their knowledge in the process of transforming the organization.

Effective Communication: This involves explaining why there is need for change as well as its advantages thus developing trust and engagement within team members.

Adaptability: Flexibility and adaptability in an uncertain situation should entail a shift in strategies or methods when necessary.

Leaders who are willing to embrace change can build a positive organizational climate that fosters continuous improvement and embraces emerging opportunities. Focusing on collaboration, agility, and innovation helps organizations navigate through transformative processes and achieve long-term success.

Building a Resilient Team in Times of Change

In times of change, it is critical to construct a resilient team that will help the organization overcome any challenges that may come its way. A resilient team will be able to adjust, create anew, and thrive under uncertainty and disruption. For this reason, leaders must be deliberate in their efforts to promote resilience and adaptability among their teams during periods of change.

Below are some methods leaders can use for building resilience among their teams:

Encourage open communication: Establishing an open-communication culture where team members feel free enough to share their minds as well as concerns enhances the exchange of different perspectives leading towards team resiliency by means of collaborative problem solving.

Promote growth mindset: Within the team, stress need for continuous learning as well as personal development. Urge employees to see change as an opportunity for growth rather than something they should resist.

Nurture emotional intelligence: Assist your teammates in developing emotional intelligence so as to enable them manage stress levels more effectively, form productive relationships with others while still being able to handle difficult situations more empathetically without compromising on resilience.

Empower decision-making: Leaders can delegate decision-making authority within the group thus allowing the members get involved actively in contributing towards achieving group goals thereby fostering autonomy and resilience due trust bestowed upon such individuals by feeling valued or appreciated.

Foster supportive environment: Make sure that your team feels secure enough take risks without fear of mistakes while learning from those mistakes. It is also important therefore that you help create a culture of collaboration whereby people support each other hence promoting development of resilience and adaptability among the team members.

By implementing these strategies, leaders can lay the foundation for a resilient team capable of navigating the complexities of change. Resilient teams do not just survive change, but they thrive by embracing new opportunities and delivering success in the face of uncertainty.

Communicating Effectively in Times of Change

During times of change, effective communication is instrumental in leading teams and organizations through the transformation process. It ensures clarity, transparency, and engagement, fostering a shared understanding and commitment to the desired outcomes. Leaders can use several strategies to communicate effectively during periods of change:

Be Transparent: Openly share information about the change, its reasons, and the expected impact. Transparency builds trust and helps alleviate uncertainty among team members.

Listen Actively: Encourage open dialogue where your team will freely express their opinions as you actively listen to them. Create an environment that makes everybody feel heard-and valued.

Use Multiple Channels: Utilize diverse communication channels to reach a wider audience and accommodate different preferences. This could be done via emails, meetings or intranet platforms even instant messaging tools (IM).

Craft Clear Messages: Develop concise and straightforward messages that clearly convey the purpose, benefits, and expectations of the change. Do not use jargon or complicated language that may cause confusion.

Provide Context: Help your employees see beyond their tasks how this change relates with broader organizational goals; then place this particular transition within that larger framework…

Proactively anticipate concerns and potential questions or resistance from your team. Respond honestly and with empathy to address fears and doubts.

Keep everybody informed through regular updates on the progress of change. This also helps maintain the state of awareness.

There is a powerful way that leaders can empower their teams, foster ownership, and ensure everyone is aligned and working towards a successful transformation – efficient communication during times of change.

Leading by example can be an incredible tactic for inspiring change as well as personal transformation. Actually, we are all catalysts for change as leaders when we embody values and behaviors in our organizations and expect our teams to follow suit. This effect creates more changes whose meaning can easily be seen in others who act similarly.

Another effective approach is showing the way by transforming ourselves first before others could be motivated to follow suit (Perttula).

If these qualities are desired in our teams, then leading by example will require us to show them ourselves first (Yukl 67). We inspire others to do things likewise by taking the initiative ourselves through being responsible for actions performed by us.

Moreover, there are other ways in which leading by example can be utilized as a tool for effective communication (Bennis 2003)

To create a culture of personal transformation, we have to be transparent in our communication. We must share our visions, goals and expectations with our team members. By clearly articulating the reasons behind the change and the benefits it will bring, we create a sense of purpose and alignment. A culture where employees feel listened to and cared for is built through active listening and empathy; this promotes trust and collaboration among them. Encourage personal growth by leading through example.

"Walk your talk."

To give everyone else the grounds as to why this change has to happen as well as its benefits, it is important that explaining such details would create a sense of direction.

Leading by example inspires change through personal transformation within ourselves (Kotter 107). This enables our teams to embrace change which leads them into their own personal growth as well (Longenecker).

Overcoming Resistence to Change

The major challenge most leaders face is overcoming resistance to change on any transformative journey. Successful implementation requires careful planning and effective strategies aimed at overcoming these challenges head on .This section therefore looks at ways in which resistance can be addressed directly leading to smooth transition that eventually results in successful implementation.

Effective communication is one of the most important strategies for overcoming resistance to change. The leaders must explain clearly why the change has been made and how it will be of benefit to everyone involved, as well as relate it to the organization's goals. This promotes employee awareness of reasons behind change, which helps to reduce resistance and increase confidence in management.

Involving employees in decision-making enables them to gain commitment and buy-in into the proposed changes. Such an approach allows employees to share ideas, perspectives and concerns that come with ownership feelings hence generating a sense of empowerment towards their job areas.. When listened to or included in the decision making process ,staff are more likely to accept and become loyal towards new ideas.

Creating a Supportive Environment for Change:

An enabling environment is instrumental in overcoming resistance to change where managers will need innovation, testing culture and be able to facilitate continuous learning processes among their staff members. Resources provision together with training programs plus mentoring facilitates employees' adjustment through development of necessary transition skills consequently boosting successful implementation of organizational transformation. Further, upon recognizing all these initiatives along its path can improve team spirit hence motivating workers towards embracing change.

Addressing Concerns and Providing Support:

Leaders should address any issues raised by employees during implementation stage since they are crucial at that juncture., Managers listening attentively while showing empathy help individuals understand their personal apprehensions about transformation efforts eventually facilitating its accomplishment via coaching guidance apart from other relevant backbones thus averting much harder shift.

Monitoring and Evaluating Progress:

Checking progress on regular basis aids top management keep track on any roadblocks or opposition that may arise from different departments related with this particular program as they are also looking forward for suggestions coming from those responsible parties who implement that improvement measure at work place otherwise can give a feedback after having identified wrong steps undertaken necessitating necessary adjustments for realization process success.

These strategies will help leaders create an environment that supports successful implementation by overcoming resistance to change. By employing effective communication, employee engagement, supporting culture, addressing concerns and monitoring progress, leaders will have paved the way for a smooth and successful transformation.

Empowering and Engaging Teams During Transformation

Teams can be empowered and engaged in order to facilitate successful transformation. Collaborative environment is created by engaging employees in the process of decision making with a sense of ownership.

Here are some strategies to enhance employee involvement and engagement during the transformation:

Clear Communication: Team members want to know what is happening and why. Leaders should keep their teams informed about progress toward their goals as well as changes in direction. This helps them see that their opinions matter and they can trust those they work with.

Open and Inclusive Decision-Making: Encourage team members' participation in decision-making forums at all times. This can be done through brainstorming sessions or feedback mechanisms within which group discussions are held. When diverse viewpoints are heard from unfamiliar sources ,they become more knowledgeable about what may have not worked out before hence leaders come up with better decisions.

Encourage Collaboration: Create opportunities for collaboration and teamwork. A sharing culture where ideas, information, resources flow freely has to be embraced.Experts advocate setting up knowledge-sharing platforms besides developing cross-functional projects or organizing team building activities like retreats/ workshops.

Provide Autonomy: Team members thrive when given autonomy over their own work; empowering them to make decisions based on trust results into greater initiative among them who then take a risk-oriented approach while carrying out their mandate .

Recognize and Reward: Make sure you acknowledge and appreciate the contributions team members make. Recognize their efforts, celebrate milestones, reward outstanding performance. This approach boosts morale while reiterating the significance of their role in the transformation process.

Engaging and empowering teams during transformation is important because it instills a sense of purpose and meaning. Employees who feel valued, involved, and motivated are more likely to embrace change, contribute their best efforts, and drive the organization towards successful outcomes.

Managing Change: Skills & Competencies for Transformational Leadership

In today's rapidly changing business landscape, organizations must be effective in managing change and possessing transformational leadership to survive constant shifts and disruptions. Leaders need various skills and competencies that ensure easy sailing through change as well as inspiring others to transform.

Problem-Solving: Change often presents complex challenges that require leaders to think critically in order to come up with innovative solutions. Problem-solving leaders are capable of identifying root causes of issues, developing creative strategies for resolving them, and piloting towards successful resolutions using their team.

Decision-Making: During times of change, leaders must make sound decisions quickly and effectively. They have to get relevant information from different sources; analyze options; estimate risks; consider all stakeholders. Strong decision-making ensures that leaders pick what will help achieve organizational transformation goals.

Adaptability: As business environments keep evolving, so should its leadership approaches flexible enough. They should welcome fresh ideas into their heads while embracing ambiguity by adjusting where necessary. When a leader is adaptive they give confidence hence make the teams very agile.

Emotional Intelligence: Change often brings emotional challenges such as resistance or uncertainty among others. Leaders who possess a high level of emotional intelligence can manage their emotions well whilst showing sympathy with other colleagues within their teams too .This skill improves communication and fosters trust building engagement during periods when going through transformations.

Developing these skills and competencies requires continuous learning as well as self-reflections. For that reason, leaders may be engaged in professional development programs, seek mentors or coaches feedback, and apply these skills actively in their day-to-day leadership roles. By sharpening their change management and transformational leadership abilities, they create a culture of adaptability to implement successful changes within an organization.

Navigating Uncertainty: Strategies for Leading Through Ambiguity

In today's fast changing business world, uncertainty accompanied by unpredictability is the order of the day. To do this effectively requires strategic planning approaches as well as honed leadership skills which can easily adapt to it. The road through ambiguity calls on leaders to use strategies that enable them make informed decisions while leading teams with confidence. Embrace the Unknown: Rather than fearing uncertainty, successful leaders embrace it as an opportunity for growth and innovation. By creating a culture that embraces change and welcomes experimentation, leaders can unlock the potential of their teams and move through ambiguous situations more quickly.

Foster Effective Communication: In times of uncertainty, clear and open communication become crucial for any leader. Leaders who maintain an open line of communication are able to clarify issues when necessary , share information between different sections , address any concerns or questions that might arise . Regular team updates town hall meetings one-on-one conversations will also help ease anxiety and build trust.

The quicker leaders can encourage others to collaborate the better because there is more at stake when conditions are ambiguous. By promoting collaboration across functions and perspectives, leaders can engage collective intellectual resources leading to creative ideas. A platform for teamwork and sharing of knowledge will provide a way for teams to operate in ambiguity.

Develop Emotional Intelligence

Leading through ambiguity means that leaders must be emotionally intelligent enough to control their emotions and stay calm under pressure. Leaders can use emotional intelligence to make their way through uncertainty while giving confidence as well as support to their team members. Active listening, empathy, and self-awareness are all components of emotional intelligence.

Continuously Learn and Adapt

Leaders must be adaptable and ready to learn in uncertain situations. Leaders who remain curious, seek feedback, and encourage growth mindsets can view ambiguity as an opportunity for learning and development. Continuous learning and adaptation support informed decision-making by leaders with regard to guiding their teams effectively.

Provide Clarity and Direction

When things are unclear due to ambiguousness, it is vital for leaders to bring clarity in order for them to set a new direction for subordinates.By setting goals, establishing priorities, assigning responsibilities effectively, leaders will steer their teams through turbulent periods.Expected behavior patterns within the groups should be made clear so that members find it easy during such tough times.

By using these techniques and methods it's possible for leadersto maintain confidence in navigating uncertainty while carrying out one's role of managing his/her team in uncertain circumstances.The ability of leadership on ambiguity has become an essential requirement towards today's leader who wants successful transformations that would result into a flexible organization which responds positively whenever change occurs.

Sustaining Change: Ensuring Long-Term Success And Adaptability

In order to achieve long-term success of an organization, it is imperative that changes are sustained efficiently.Sustaining change seeks not only after implementing initial transformation strategies but also how the same has been integrated into the culture of the organization.

In this part, we will discuss some effective growth strategies and methods that leaders should use to succeed in the long run and become adaptable to future changes.

One essential step to sustaining change is the establishment of a culture of continuous improvement. In addition, leaders need to cultivate a mindset of agility and innovative thinking and offer empowerment to employees substituting socialism for capitalist-market thinking in order to allow new ideas to take root in uncertain places as they emerge. Through promoting an environment and a culture favorable to trying things out, learning enterprises--defined as those with less than 1000 employees--can temper judgment by learning what is actually successful before making changes. Thus organizations will have greater adaptability, embracing change before it arrives.

Next, maintaining open communications is essential to supporting change. Leaders need to make sure employees have multiple channels through which they can voice their feedback or worries and participate in the process of decision-making. By having employees go through the change, organizations can gradually stimulate a sense of responsibility and commitment. In this way the chances of long-term success are significantly increased.

Lastly, to maintain change calls for frequent assessment as well as a re-evaluation of the effects from changes made. Through data collection and monitoring progress, leaders can see where improvements should be made or the course must be adjusted. This forward-looking approach enables organizations to anticipate potential issues early on and make corrections as needed for lasting success.

Chapter **12**

Strategic Decision-Making

Welcome to Chapter 12 of "Leader's Anchor Ship". In this chapter, we will explore the fascinating world of strategic decision-making and how it can enhance your business's competitive edge. Making effective strategic decisions is crucial for staying ahead in today's dynamic and competitive business landscape.

By diving into the depths of strategic decision-making, you will gain valuable insights and expert analysis on how to navigate the complexities of the business world. We will provide you with the tools and knowledge to make informed choices that align with your business goals, identify opportunities, mitigate risks, and drive success.

Whether you are an aspiring entrepreneur or an experienced business leader, this chapter will equip you with the necessary skills to develop a robust strategic decision-making framework. We will guide you through analyzing market trends, understanding the competitive landscape, evaluating alternatives, and making well-informed decisions.

Furthermore, we will explore the importance of implementing and executing strategic decisions effectively, monitoring their progress, and evaluating their outcomes. We will also delve into the need to adapt your decision-making process in a rapidly changing environment and provide industry-specific insights to help you navigate your particular field.

Finally, we will examine real-life case studies of successful strategic decision-making and explore the future trends and innovations that will shape decision-making practices in the years to come. Are you ready to enhance your business's competitive edge through the power of strategic decision-making? Let's embark on this exciting journey together!

Understanding the Importance of Strategic Decision-Making

Strategic decision-making plays a pivotal role in driving business success and maintaining a competitive edge. By making informed choices based on careful analysis and planning, companies can navigate challenges and capitalize on opportunities in an ever-changing marketplace.

So, why is strategic decision-making so important? Here are some key reasons:

Forward-thinking approach: Strategic decision-making involves considering the long-term implications of every choice. By taking a proactive and forward-thinking stance, businesses can anticipate future trends and position themselves for sustainable growth.

Enhanced resource allocation: Making strategic decisions allows companies to allocate their resources effectively. By focusing on high-priority initiatives that align with their core objectives, organizations can optimize their investments and maximize returns.

Risk mitigation: Strategic decision-making involves assessing potential risks and developing contingency plans. By carefully evaluating the potential consequences of different choices, businesses can minimize risks and mitigate their impact on operations.

Competitive advantage: Businesses that excel in strategic decision-making often gain a competitive edge over their rivals. By identifying unique opportunities, capitalizing on emerging trends, and adapting swiftly to market changes, companies can stay ahead of the curve and outperform their competitors.

Alignment with goals: Each strategic decision is made with the overarching goals of the business in mind. By ensuring alignment with the company's mission, vision, and values, organizations can pursue opportunities that propel them closer to their desired outcomes.

Understanding the importance of strategic decision-making is the first step towards harnessing its power. By recognizing its benefits and advantages, businesses can create a roadmap for success, embrace innovation, and thrive in a dynamic business landscape.

Developing a Strategic Decision-Making Framework

In order to make effective strategic decisions for your business, it is essential to develop a robust decision-making framework. This framework acts as a guide, providing a structured approach to decision-making that is tailored to your business's specific needs.

Identify Your Objectives: Begin by clearly defining your business's objectives and goals. Understanding what you want to achieve will help you make decisions that align with your overarching strategy. Gather Relevant Information: Collect and analyze data and information that is relevant to the decision at hand. This could include market research, industry trends, and competitor analysis. Assess Risks and Opportunities: Evaluate the potential risks and opportunities associated with each decision. This step helps you weigh the potential benefits against the potential drawbacks.

Consider Alternatives: Explore different alternatives and options that could address your business's objectives. This allows you to consider a range of possibilities before making a final decision. Evaluate and Compare: Assess each alternative based on predetermined criteria, such as cost, feasibility, and alignment with your strategic goals. This will help you identify the best option.Make the Decision: Once you have evaluated and compared all the alternatives, make a well-informed decision. Trust in the process and the data gathered to guide your choice.

Create an Action Plan: Develop a detailed action plan outlining the steps required to implement the decision effectively. This plan should include timelines, resource allocation, and key responsibilities.

By following a comprehensive strategic decision-making framework, you can ensure that your decisions are well-informed, aligned with your business goals, and capable of driving meaningful outcomes. This structured approach enhances your decision-making process, leading to more successful outcomes for your business.

Analyzing Market Trends and Competitive Landscape

When it comes to strategic decision-making, analyzing market trends and understanding the competitive landscape is crucial for business success. By gaining insights into these factors, businesses can make informed choices and gain a competitive edge in the market.

Market trends provide valuable information about the direction in which an industry is headed. By identifying and analyzing these trends, businesses can anticipate customer preferences, emerging technologies, and shifts in demand. This proactive approach allows companies to adjust their strategies accordingly and stay ahead in a rapidly changing market.

- Identify emerging customer needs and preferences
- Anticipate industry-specific challenges and opportunities
- Stay updated with technological advancements
- Adapt strategies to meet evolving market demands

Understanding the competitive landscape is equally important. By assessing the strengths, weaknesses, opportunities, and threats posed by competitors, businesses can make strategic decisions that give them an upper hand. A thorough competitive landscape analysis helps companies identify gaps in the market that they can exploit and identify potential threats that they need to address.

- Evaluate competitors' product offerings
- Assess competitors' marketing and branding strategies
- Analyze competitors' customer base and target market
- Identify competitors' pricing and distribution strategies
- By analyzing market trends and the competitive landscape, businesses can make informed decisions that align with their goals and give them a competitive advantage. Stay tuned for the next section, where we will delve into the process of identifying strategic opportunities and risks.

Identifying Strategic Opportunities and Risks

When it comes to strategic decision-making, one of the key tasks is to identify the strategic opportunities and risks that can significantly impact the success of your business. By thoroughly assessing these factors, you can make informed choices that align with your business goals and enhance your competitive edge.

To identify strategic opportunities, it is essential to stay updated on market trends, industry developments, and emerging technologies. By understanding the changing landscape and recognizing potential growth areas, you can seize new opportunities and gain a competitive advantage.

On the other hand, strategic risks are potential threats that may hinder the achievement of your business objectives. These risks can arise from various factors such as market volatility, economic uncertainties, regulatory changes, or technological disruptions. By identifying and assessing these risks, you can develop strategies to mitigate their impact and proactively respond to challenges.

To effectively identify strategic opportunities and risks, conducting a thorough risk assessment is crucial. A risk assessment involves evaluating the likelihood and potential impact of various risks on your business. This evaluation allows you to prioritize risks and allocate resources accordingly, ensuring that you address the most critical vulnerabilities first.

During the risk assessment process, it is important to involve key stakeholders from different departments and levels of your organization. Their unique perspectives and expertise can contribute valuable insights to the risk assessment, enabling a comprehensive understanding of the strategic landscape.

When conducting a risk assessment, consider utilizing proven methodologies such as SWOT analysis (Strengths, Weaknesses, Opportunities, and Threats) or PESTLE analysis (Political, Economic, Sociocultural, Technological, Legal, and Environmental factors). These frameworks provide structured approaches for identifying and assessing strategic risks, ensuring a systematic and holistic evaluation.

- Identify and assess potential strategic opportunities.
- Stay updated on market trends and industry developments.
- Evaluate the potential impact of emerging technologies.
- Analyze market volatility, economic uncertainties, and regulatory changes.
- Engage key stakeholders from different departments and levels of the organization.
- Utilize methodologies such as SWOT analysis or PESTLE analysis for a systematic evaluation.
- By identifying strategic opportunities and risks through a comprehensive risk assessment, you can make informed decisions that maximize the potential for success and navigate potential challenges with confidence. With this strategic approach, your

business can stay agile, adapt to evolving market conditions, and maintain a competitive advantage.

Evaluating Alternatives and Making Informed Decisions

When it comes to strategic decision-making, evaluating alternatives is a crucial step in the process. By thoroughly considering different options, you can make informed decisions that align with your business goals and maximize the chances of success.

Here are some effective techniques to help you evaluate alternatives and make well-informed decisions:

Weigh the Pros and Cons: Make a list of the advantages and disadvantages of each alternative. Consider how each option aligns with your business objectives, potential risks involved, and the impact on various stakeholders.

- Consider Risks and Rewards: Assess the potential risks associated with each alternative and the potential rewards they offer. Evaluate the likelihood of success, possible challenges, and the long-term implications of your decision.
- Utilize Decision-Making Tools: Employ decision-making tools such as cost-benefit analysis, SWOT analysis, or decision matrices to evaluate alternatives objectively. These tools can provide a structured approach to weigh different factors and make comparisons.
- Seek Expert Advice: Consult with subject matter experts or professionals who can offer valuable insights and expertise in evaluating alternatives. Their knowledge and experience can provide a fresh perspective and help you make more informed decisions.
- Consider Long-Term Implications: Look beyond short-term gains and consider the long-term implications of each alternative. Evaluate how your decision will impact your business in the future and its ability to adapt to changing market conditions.

By following these techniques, you can evaluate alternatives effectively and make decisions that are backed by thorough analysis and understanding. Remember, the goal is to choose the best strategic course of action that will propel your business forward.

Implementing and Executing Strategic Decisions

Implementing and executing strategic decisions can pose significant challenges for businesses. It requires careful planning, effective communication, and diligent monitoring to ensure successful implementation. Here, we will explore the key considerations and strategies involved in implementing strategic decisions, providing you with valuable insights to navigate this complex process.

Clearly Define the Strategic Decisions: Before implementing any strategic decision, it is crucial to have a clear understanding of what needs to be achieved and why it is important for your business. This step involves defining the objectives, goals, and desired outcomes of the decision.

Develop an Action Plan: Once the strategic decisions are defined, it is essential to develop a detailed action plan. This plan should outline the specific tasks, responsibilities, timelines, and resources required to execute the decisions effectively.

Establish Effective Communication Channels: Communication plays a vital role in successfully implementing strategic decisions. It is important to establish clear channels of communication and ensure that all relevant stakeholders are informed about the decisions, their roles, and the expected outcomes. Regular communication and feedback mechanisms will help address any concerns and ensure alignment throughout the implementation process.

Monitor Progress and Adapt as Needed: Effective monitoring is critical to evaluate the progress and success of the implemented decisions. Regularly track and measure key performance indicators to identify any deviations from the desired outcomes. If necessary, adapt and adjust the implementation plan to address any unforeseen challenges or changes in the business environment.

Implementing and executing strategic decisions requires careful planning, effective communication, and diligent monitoring. By following these key strategies and considerations, businesses can enhance their ability to translate strategic decisions into successful outcomes.

Monitoring and Evaluating Strategic Decisions

Once strategic decisions have been implemented, it is essential to monitor and evaluate their effectiveness to ensure optimal outcomes for your business. Monitoring strategic decisions allows you to track progress, measure success, and identify areas that may require adjustments. Evaluating decisions helps you gain valuable insights into the impact of your choices and determine areas for improvement.

Here are some key steps to effectively monitor and evaluate strategic decisions:

1. Establish Key Performance Indicators (KPIs): Define measurable metrics that align with your business goals and reflect the outcomes you seek to achieve. These KPIs will serve as benchmarks to evaluate the success of your strategic decisions.
2. Collect Data: Gather relevant data and information to monitor the performance and outcomes associated with your strategic decisions. This may include financial data, customer feedback, market trends, or other performance indicators.
3. Analyze Results: Use data analysis techniques and tools to assess the impact of your strategic decisions. Compare actual results against your established KPIs to determine whether you have achieved your desired outcomes.
4. Identify Areas for Improvement: Analyze the data to identify areas where your strategic decisions may have fallen short or could be optimized. This analysis will help you uncover opportunities for improvement and formulate actionable strategies.
5. Make Necessary Adjustments: Based on your evaluation, make any necessary adjustments to your strategic decisions. This may involve refining your approach, reallocating resources, or implementing new measures to enhance performance.

Remember that monitoring and evaluating strategic decisions is an iterative process. By continuously assessing their effectiveness, you can strengthen your decision-making capabilities and drive sustainable business growth.

Adapting to Change and Revising Strategic Decision-Making

Strategic decision-making is a dynamic process that requires constant adaptation to changes in the business environment. In order to stay competitive and ensure long-term success, businesses must be agile and responsive to emerging opportunities and challenges.

When faced with new market trends, technological advancements, or shifts in customer preferences, it becomes imperative to revise previous decisions and strategies. This flexibility enables businesses to capitalize on emerging opportunities and mitigate potential risks.

Here are some key steps to adapt to change and revise strategic decisions:

Regularly assess the business environment: Continuously monitor market conditions, industry trends, and customer demands to stay informed about changes that may impact your previous decisions. Gather feedback and insights: Seek input from stakeholders, employees, and customers to gain valuable perspectives and identify areas where adaptation is necessary.

Reevaluate assumptions and data: Review the assumptions and data that formed the basis of your initial decision. If new information emerges, revise your analysis accordingly.

Consider alternative options: Explore alternative strategies and courses of action that may be better suited to the changing business landscape.

Communicate and engage: Keep key stakeholders informed about the need for changes to strategic decisions. Seek their input and involvement to ensure alignment and commitment.

Monitor outcomes: Continuously evaluate the outcomes of revised decisions to assess their effectiveness. Make further adjustments if necessary. By embracing change and being open to revising decisions, businesses can adapt to evolving circumstances and maintain a competitive edge in the marketplace. This proactive approach allows for strategic agility and positions the business for long-term success.

Strategic Decision-Making in Different Industries

Strategic decision-making is a critical process that every business must undertake to secure a competitive advantage. However, the considerations and challenges faced in this process can vary significantly across different industries. Each industry has its unique characteristics and dynamics that influence strategic decision-making.

By examining strategic decision-making in various industries, we can gain valuable insights into industry-specific approaches and best practices. These insights can enhance our decision-making capabilities and help us navigate the complexities of our respective industries.

Here are some key industry-specific considerations to keep in mind:

Technology: In the fast-paced world of technology, strategic decision-making revolves around innovation, market disruptions, and rapid changes in consumer demands. Companies in this industry must continuously assess emerging technologies, anticipate trends, and adapt their strategies accordingly.

Healthcare: The healthcare industry is heavily regulated and constantly evolving. Strategic decision-making in healthcare requires deep understanding of compliance requirements, patient needs, and technological advancements. It also involves assessing risks and benefits associated with treatment options and medical breakthroughs.

Finance: Financial institutions face unique challenges related to risk management, regulatory compliance, and market volatility. Strategic decision-making in the finance industry involves assessing market trends, evaluating investment opportunities, and managing potential risks to ensure long-term stability and profitability.

Retail: Retail businesses focus on consumer behavior, market trends, and competitive pricing strategies. Strategic decision-making in the retail industry involves analyzing consumer preferences, optimizing supply chain management, and adapting to ever-changing market dynamics.

Manufacturing: Manufacturers must make strategic decisions related to production processes, supply chain optimization, and product innovation. Decision-making in this industry involves evaluating cost efficiencies, sustainability practices, and technological advancements to deliver quality products while staying competitive.

These are just a few examples of how strategic decision-making differs across industries. By understanding the nuances and challenges specific to our industry, we can make more informed and effective decisions that drive growth and success.

Future Trends and Innovations in Strategic Decision-Making

The constantly evolving business landscape calls for new strategies and approaches in strategic decision-making. As we look to the future, several emerging trends and innovations are set to shape the way businesses make critical choices to stay competitive and drive growth.

One key future trend is the increasing integration of artificial intelligence (AI) and machine learning (ML) in decision-making processes. These technologies have the potential to analyze vast amounts of data, identify patterns, and provide valuable insights that can inform strategic decisions. By leveraging AI and ML, businesses can make more data-driven and accurate choices, enhancing their overall decision-making capabilities.

Another significant innovation is the rise of predictive analytics in strategic decision-making. With the power of predictive analytics, businesses can forecast future outcomes based on historical data, market trends, and various variables. This allows organizations to anticipate potential risks and opportunities, enabling more proactive and strategic decision-making.

Furthermore, the increasing emphasis on sustainability and social responsibility is expected to influence decision-making practices. Businesses are recognizing the importance of integrating environmental, social, and governance (ESG) factors into their decision-making frameworks. By considering the long-term impact of their choices on the planet, people, and profitability, organizations can align their strategic decisions with sustainable practices and meet evolving consumer demands.

Chapter 13

Talent Development and Succession Planning

In this chapter, we will explore the vital topics of talent development and succession planning. These strategies are crucial for ensuring the long-term success and sustainability of your organization.

Talent development involves identifying, nurturing, and enhancing the skills and capabilities of your employees. It is an essential aspect of building a skilled and effective workforce that can adapt to the ever-changing business landscape. Succession planning, on the other hand, focuses on preparing future leaders who can seamlessly step into key roles when the need arises.

By investing in talent development and succession planning, you not only enhance the capabilities of individual employees but also create a strong pipeline of potential leaders. This proactive approach ensures a smooth transition of crucial roles and maintains organizational stability.

Throughout this chapter, we will delve into the intricacies of talent development and succession planning, exploring various strategies, best practices, and practical steps to implement these initiatives successfully.

So, let's embark on the journey to unleash the potential of your employees and pave the way for a bright future for your organization. Are you ready to unlock the power of talent development and succession planning? Let's get started!

Understanding Talent Development

In today's competitive business landscape, talent development plays a crucial role in driving long-term success for organizations. It encompasses a range of strategies and practices aimed at identifying, nurturing, and enhancing the skills and abilities of employees.

Effective talent development programs not only enable individuals to reach their full potential but also contribute to organizational growth and productivity. By investing in the development of their workforce, companies can build a pool of highly skilled and motivated employees who are capable of taking on new challenges and driving innovation.

To promote talent development within your organization, it is essential to adopt a comprehensive approach. Here are some key strategies and best practices to consider:

1. **Identify Talent:** Begin by identifying individuals who show promise and potential within your organization. This can be done through performance evaluations, talent assessments, and feedback from managers and colleagues.

2. **Nurture Growth:** Once identified, it is crucial to provide employees with the necessary resources and opportunities to enhance their skills. This can include training programs, mentorship initiatives, and job rotations.

3. **Foster a Learning Culture:** Create an environment that encourages continuous learning and professional development. This can be achieved through promoting knowledge-sharing, providing access to online learning platforms, and supporting employees in pursuing further education.
4. **Offer Career Advancement Opportunities:** Provide clear paths for career progression within your organization. This can involve creating performance-based promotion criteria, offering challenging assignments, and creating leadership development programs.
5. **Recognize and Reward Achievement:** Acknowledge and reward employees who consistently demonstrate exceptional performance. This can help boost motivation, morale, and loyalty within your workforce.

By implementing these strategies and best practices, organizations can create a culture of talent development that not only attracts and retains top talent but also drives continuous growth and success.

Benefits of an Effective Succession Planning

Implementing a well-designed succession plan brings numerous benefits to your organization. It serves as a strategic tool that ensures a smooth transition of key roles, preventing disruptions and maintaining organizational stability.

Here are some of the key benefits of a robust succession plan:

Talent retention: A succession plan demonstrates your commitment to employee growth and development. It motivates talented individuals to stay with your organization, knowing that their hard work and dedication will be recognized and rewarded in the form of future leadership opportunities.

Reduced risk: Succession planning mitigates the risks associated with unexpected departures or retirements of key personnel. By identifying and grooming potential successors, you ensure a seamless transition, minimizing the potential impact on business operations.

Continuity of leadership: A well-defined succession plan ensures a smooth transfer of knowledge, skills, and expertise from outgoing leaders to their successors. This continuity of leadership allows for the preservation of institutional knowledge and guarantees organizational stability.

Preparedness for change: Succession planning prepares your organization for any future changes in leadership, whether it be due to retirement, expansion, or unforeseen circumstances. It allows you to proactively develop a pipeline of capable leaders who can take on new challenges and drive the organization forward.

Increased employee engagement: When employees see opportunities for growth and advancement within the organization, they become more engaged and motivated. A well-executed succession plan fosters a culture of continuous learning, empowerment, and career progression.

By investing in succession planning, you strengthen your organization's talent pool, enhance employee satisfaction, and build a solid foundation for long-term success.

Identifying Potential Leaders

Identifying individuals with leadership potential is a crucial step in the succession planning process. By recognizing employees who possess the necessary qualities and skills for future leadership positions, organizations can ensure a smooth transition and secure their long-term success.

There are various methods and assessments that can help identify potential leaders within your organization:

Performance Evaluation: Reviewing employee performance can provide valuable insights into their ability to take on leadership roles. Look for consistent high performance, strong problem-solving skills, and the ability to motivate and inspire others.

Assessment Centers: These centers can be useful for evaluating leadership potential through role-plays, simulations, and psychometric tests. They provide a holistic view of an employee's capabilities and behaviors in various scenarios.

360-Degree Feedback: Collect feedback from peers, subordinates, and supervisors to gain a comprehensive understanding of an employee's leadership skills and potential areas for improvement. This multi-perspective approach can provide valuable insights. Another effective way to identify potential leaders is by looking for individuals who display certain characteristics and behaviors commonly associated with effective leaders:

Initiative: Look for employees who take the initiative to identify and solve problems. They display a proactive attitude and show a willingness to go beyond their assigned responsibilities.

Adaptability: Effective leaders are adaptable and embrace change. Look for employees who can quickly adjust to new situations, learn from challenges, and find innovative solutions.

Communications Skills: Strong communication skills are essential for leadership. Identify employees who can clearly articulate their ideas, listen actively, and collaborate effectively with others.

By utilizing these methods and assessing specific qualities, organizations can identify and develop potential leaders who will drive the future growth and success of the business.

Developing Leadership Skills

Investing in the growth and development of potential leaders is crucial for the long-term success of your organization. By providing opportunities to develop leadership skills, you can empower your employees to take on greater responsibilities and contribute to the growth of your company.

Approaches to Developing Leadership Skills

There are various approaches you can take to develop the leadership skills of your employees:
Mentorship Programs: Pairing potential leaders with experienced mentors can provide guidance and help them learn from seasoned professionals.

Training Workshops: Conducting workshops on leadership techniques and strategies allows employees to learn and apply new skills in a supportive environment.

Stretch Assignments: Assigning challenging projects or tasks to potential leaders gives them the opportunity to expand their skill set and gain valuable experience.

Leadership Development Programs

Implementing structured leadership development programs can greatly enhance the growth of your potential leaders. These programs typically include:

Leadership Training: Providing specialized training sessions that cover a wide range of leadership competencies and skills.

Executive Coaching: Engaging professional coaches to provide one-on-one guidance and support tailored to the unique needs of each potential leader.

Networking Opportunities: Encouraging interactions with senior leaders and industry experts through events, conferences, and networking sessions.

By combining these approaches and programs, you can create a comprehensive development plan that nurtures the leadership skills of your employees and prepares them for future leadership roles within your organization.

Creating a Succession Plan

A well-defined succession plan is crucial for organizations looking to ensure a seamless transition of leadership. By creating a comprehensive succession plan tailored to your organization's specific needs and goals, you can lay a solid foundation for future success.

To create an effective succession plan, follow these steps:

Identify key positions: Start by identifying the key positions within your organization that require succession planning. These positions are critical to the functioning and success of your business.

Assess current talent: Evaluate the skills, capabilities, and potential of your current employees. Look for individuals who exhibit strong leadership qualities and have the ability to take up key roles in the future.

Develop a talent pool: Build a pipeline of potential successors by offering training, mentoring, and development opportunities. This will ensure that the right individuals are prepared to step into leadership positions should the need arise.

Create development plans: Tailor development plans for each potential successor to address their specific areas for growth. Provide them with opportunities to acquire the skills, knowledge, and experiences necessary for success in their future roles.

Establish clear criteria: Define the criteria and competencies required for individuals to be considered for key roles in the succession plan. This will help you evaluate candidates objectively and make informed decisions.

Implement mentorship programs: Pair potential successors with experienced leaders within your organization. This mentorship can provide valuable guidance and support as they prepare for their future roles.

Monitor and adjust: Continuously monitor the progress of your succession plan and make any necessary adjustments along the way. Regularly review and update the plan to reflect changes in organizational needs and the development of potential successors. By following these steps and creating a robust succession plan, your organization can ensure continuity, maintain stability, and be prepared for future leadership transitions.

Implementing and Maintaining Talent Development Programs

Implementing talent development programs is a crucial step in fostering growth and success within your organization. To ensure their effectiveness, it is essential to approach this process thoughtfully and strategically.

Here are some key insights to help you design and implement effective talent development programs:

Define clear objectives: Clearly define the goals and objectives of your talent development programs. Identify the specific skills, competencies, and behaviors you want to develop in your employees.

Customize programs: Tailor your talent development programs to meet the unique needs and challenges of your organization. Consider the current skill gaps, future business requirements, and individual employee development plans.

Secure necessary resources: Ensure you have the financial and logistical resources needed to support your talent development programs. This may include budget allocation, access to training materials, tools, and technology.

Engage stakeholders: Involve key stakeholders such as executives, managers, and employees in the design and implementation process. Seek their input and gain their buy-in to foster a culture of continuous learning and development.

Maintaining momentum and long-term success:

Monitor progress: Regularly monitor and evaluate the progress of your talent development programs. Use key performance indicators (KPIs) and feedback mechanisms to measure the effectiveness of the programs and make necessary adjustments.

Promote a learning culture: Create an environment that values continuous learning and development. Encourage employees to take ownership of their development and provide opportunities for ongoing education and training.

Recognize and reward: Acknowledge and reward employees who actively participate in talent development programs and demonstrate growth and improvement. This reinforces the importance of continuous learning and motivates others to engage in the programs.

Adapt and evolve: Stay agile and adapt your talent development programs to changing business needs and industry trends. Continuously seek feedback from employees and stakeholders to ensure your programs remain relevant and effective.

Evaluating Succession Planning Strategies

Regular evaluation of your succession planning strategies is crucial to ensure their effectiveness. By evaluating your strategies, you can identify areas of improvement and make necessary adjustments to enhance your succession planning initiatives.

When evaluating succession planning strategies, consider the following methods and metrics:

Performance Metrics: Measure the performance of your successor candidates against predefined criteria to assess their readiness for leadership roles.

Feedback and Surveys: Gather feedback from stakeholders, including employees and managers, to gain insights into the effectiveness of your succession planning programs.

Talent Development Progress: Evaluate the progress of development plans for potential leaders to track their growth and identify areas for further development.

Succession Plan Execution: Assess how well your succession plan is executed, including the smoothness of transitions and the alignment of successor skills with the needs of key roles.

Succession Planning ROI: Calculate the return on investment of your succession planning efforts by analyzing the impact on organizational performance and employee engagement.

Based on the evaluation results, make informed decisions to refine and optimize your succession planning strategies. Regular evaluation ensures that your approach remains aligned with the changing needs of your organization and maximizes the potential for future success.

Ensuring Sustainability and Continuous Improvement

To build a robust future for your organization, it is crucial to focus on sustainability and continuous improvement in talent development and succession planning. Sustainability ensures that these strategies can withstand the test of time, while continuous improvement allows organizations to adapt and excel in a constantly evolving business landscape.

Sustainability in talent development and succession planning involves creating programs and practices that can be implemented and maintained over the long term. This includes aligning these strategies with your organization's core values, goals, and culture. By embedding talent development and succession planning into the fabric of your organization, you can foster a continuous cycle of growth and development.

Continuous improvement is equally important in ensuring the effectiveness of talent development and succession planning efforts. By regularly evaluating these strategies, identifying areas for improvement, and implementing changes, you can enhance the overall impact and outcomes. This includes staying up-to-date with industry trends, adopting new technologies, and embracing innovative approaches.

By prioritizing sustainability and continuous improvement, your organization can create a culture that values talent development and succession planning as an ongoing journey rather than a one-time initiative. This mindset encourages collaboration, learning, and growth at all levels of the organization, leading to increased employee engagement, retention, and overall organizational success.

Chapter 14

Developing Authentic Leadership Presence

Whether you are a new or an experienced leader, refining your leadership style and developing a strong presence can significantly contribute to your ability to inspire and lead others. Authentic leadership presence not only represents raising your presence and being driven and charismatic, but also controlling with integrity, establishing strong connections with others, and having the passion for your vision and missions. This chapter focuses on a number of tips and approaches that can help you to develop your authentic leadership presence. Starting from the basic qualities of leadership presence and ending with the sections on leadership presence and trust, communication skills, and learning emotional intelligence.

Are you looking forward to understanding how to develop your authentic leadership presence and start to make the right impact? Let's start our journey together.

Understanding Leadership Presence

Before discussing how you can develop your leadership presence, it is essential to understand what this notion means. Does being a leader presupposes having leadership presence, or people with positions of leaders may lack essential qualities of this presence? To influence others, leaders must have a number of characteristics that can make them leaders and inspire other or people, who have gathered around leaders without having these characteristics. What is it, and what are the qualities of a leader that may develop his presence and serve for the benefits of this presence?

- A leader is associated with the following qualities:
- Influence that a leader practices on others;
- The ability to motivate and control other people:
- A number of people, who gather around a leader and attempt to influence them;
- As a rule, leaders have a strong personality;
- The ability to lead people in the right direction;
- A leader must have a vision;
- A leader must be able to communicate his or her vision;
- A leader must be in charge.

The first characteristic is charisma. When discussing a person with a leadership presence, many often refer to a person who everyone feels is charismatic; in other words, this person can influence others and engage the audience. Charismatic leaders always tend to engage global audiences through creative and innovative means to allow them to realize their purpose . Accountability is when leaders are willing and can pull back and assess their genuineness. Please, performing your duties does not necessary mean pretending, it assumes the requirement of responsibility and the fulfillment of their duties time and again. The third characteristic is empathy which refers to leaders who primarily appreciate and therefore understand other people's feelings, and the feelings here are distress and excitement among others . Leaders who

have empathy as their trait can always easily figure out the departments or the areas that their workers are aggrieved. Empathy character allows each worker to demonstrate a hug and therefore support the environment. The last characteristic that I chose is adaptability and refers to the leaders always willing to shift when extraordinary circumstances. Leaders that are flexible will always be dependable in the long run. Please, remaining inflexible for every decision you make will always make you feel uncomfortable due to the slow responses of the team. If you become flexible and adaptable, your team will equally feel comfortable when you work to meet their needs and solve their complaints I decided to discuss these four characteristics because they would enable me to remain a true and notable leader towards facilitating a supply chain company . An adaptable leader can always change their ordinary ways when extraordinary circumstances arrive.

Authenticity implies that leaders are themselves and are genuine. It includes:

Aligning actions with core values in challenging situations.

Being transparent and honest.

Embracing vulnerability and admitting mistakes.

Authentic leaders create a climate of trust, empowerment to the team, and innovation and growth. Their ability to feel and connect at the human level helps to build strong relationships and facilitate the success of the organization.

Building Trust and Credibility

Establishing trust and credibility is essential for effective leadership presence. If your team and stakeholders trust you and have faith in you, they may feel more motivated and ready to take your side. The following strategies may be employed to help in this regard.

Actions speak louder than words. Being honest, ethical, transparent, and consistent in your behavior and maintaining professionalism are crucial . High ethical behavior is essential, and keeping your promises is also involved.

Effective and open communication is vital for building a connection with your team and contributes to unifying teams and aligning them in terms of goals. It can help to foster a sense of trust, build a foundation for cooperation and support among the team members, and create a safe environment for personal growth and communication.

Learn to delegate tasks to your team efficiently. Show that you have the conviction to trust them with tasks and empower them to make choices. Provide them with necessary information and subtly support them in important decisions.

Consistency in actions and communication will help to create a stable presence which can be depended upon. createState_experienced a safe spaceughspaceperiencedasspace for experienc experiencedsfe_quiet in-trigger experiencedqueuepileteam and manage experiencedspace pileexperiencedrowth and be experiencess experiencedoundationT To create a climate of tr pile_sCare pilehington experienced and let the team member query any experiencedelniling pile_a pileundsletcher and acknewlinoughtqueueledge essauxperienced queuelacheir pile_a pileundsqueued issues.

Remember, trust and credibility aren't made overnight. It takes time, effort, and a great deal of consistency to start transferring views and beliefs from one side to the other. Feel free to implement these strategies, analyzing and adapting them to your personal leadership presence and the production dynamics in your company.

Improving Leadership Communication Skills

Effective communication is vital when it comes to demonstrating your leadership presence. You might be familiar with your vision and the result you want to achieve but sharing it with your subordinates is a separate issue. To clearly explain your ideas to others and develop the necessary communication skills, learn to follow the next techniques:

Clarity and conciseness: first and foremost, share your plans and expectations clearly and thoroughly. Ensure they can be easily understood by others and avoid using jargon or a too scientific language.

Active listening: next, make sure to listen to the people around you. When you actively engage in a conversation and make the other party feel important, you build strong communication skills and relationships.

Non-verbal communication habitudes: watch your face, your voice, and the tone you are using. Besides, do not forget that a leader's position must remain open or relaxed.

Empathy and emotional intelligence: try to put yourself in the other person's place whenever you are starting a conversation. think about which words might hurt your feelings and what words will have a positive influence.

Readiness to adapt: finally, it is important to be able to adapt. Understand that different people require different approaches to communication. Also, different situations imply altering your message and its final scope.

Constructive criticism: finally, your feedback must be specific, accurate, and given in a very gentle and polite way. Thus, try to learn how you can build your team members and establish a pleasant atmosphere within the company.

Mastering your communication abilities will not only help you to demonstrate your leadership presence, but also inspire and motivate your team. Remember that successful communication is a tool that requires a constant improvement and development. Social and emotional intelligence and leadership presence

Emotional intelligence is one of the essential tools for leaders who want to develop an authentic leadership presence. It helps you connect with other staff members, builds better relationships with them and provides you with an opportunity to lead them with empathy and resilience. There are various ways to enhance your emotional intelligence:

Self-awareness : use this tool to understand how your emotions impact your decisions, behaviour and attitude. Remember about your strengths and weaknesses to be able to lead with self-awareness and honesty.

Empathy : by mastering this emotional intelligence tool you may be able to better understand other teammates, trust their vision and feelings and lead them by example.

Self-regulation : this tool is invaluable in a situation that requires you to rest calm and emotionally stable in the challenging situation. Use it to improve your own behaviour and lead with confidence.

Social and emotional intelligence is also about recognising, understanding and sharing the feelings of other people. It helps the leaders to establish better relationships, solve the arising conflicts and make the work environment better for all teams members. Mastering it also allowed you to adjust your leadership style to different types of people and situation – motivating and inspiring other staff members. It will also help you to have better chances to develop an effective decision-making process.

Leading with purpose and values

Leading with purpose and values refers to a strong sense of mission and commitment to one's core beliefs and values. Purpose refers to a sense of mission that directs actions and tends to benefit the subject in question as well as a broader stakeholder community. Leading with purpose entails creating, clarifying, and communicating a compelling, ambitious sense of purpose that one seeks to accomplish. As such, it inspires actions and efforts in such a way that one's purpose finds expression and realization in one's performance and interactions with others . Hence, a strong sense of purpose and coordination with that mission form an important aspect of leadership presence.

It is with purpose that people become alive, real, and credible. When a leader believes in a specific mission and understands why the mission exists, the mission and purpose become personified through the leader. With a purpose, leaders tend to align their actions in the organization in order to achieve their purpose and mission. Leading with purpose, therefore, helps to focus on getting things done in the organization. Purpose ensures that leaders know what to prioritize as well as the most important plan to allocate resources and time to. Thus, leaders will focus on the most critical programs and activities that will build their business or careers with a sense of passion and love as their calling. Leading with purpose guarantees that the interests of the concerned group are well catered for concerning decision-making. As a leader, leading with purpose may enhance effectiveness and success in service.

In addition, leading with values entails upholding and demonstrating one's values. Since everyone has values that he lives by, leaders must demonstrate what they stand for and are committed to. Values refer to the moral principles that guide people's behavior and serve as standards that determine the degree of accomplishment of individual as well as organizational lives. When a leader acts on his values his life and work are integrated.

Leading with values creates a culture in the organization that promotes accountability, integrity, and respect . Consequently, the leader earns the trust of his followers who are inspired to excel in their work because they know that their leader supports them. Leadership presence is about leading with purpose and values. It is not about authority or charisma, but about believing in one's mission and values. Doing this ultimately constitutes a compelling leadership presence.

Developing Executive Presence

Executive presence is critical for any leader, especially for those who want to make a difference and succeed at higher levels in an organization. It implies having confidence, poise, and influencing the way in which one interacts with others. To develop executive presence, the following strategies should be put into practice:

- Building confidence. Having confidence in one's knowledge and ability is indispensable. This confidence can be stoked by actively learning new things and ensuring that one's expertise is always up-to-date, and soliciting feedback to enhance skills.

- Showing poise. Remain calm even in the face of hardship and adversity or in high-pressure situations. Develop stress management qualities to always remain composed.

- Developing communication skills. Learn to speak persuasively and influence the audience with your speech. Being masterful in the art of influencing others will enable you to transmit short, powerful messages people will actively listen to.

- Establishing a powerful presence. Mind your physical presence, including your body language, posture, and tone of voice. These should all signal confidence, persuasiveness and a sense of command.

- Leading with vision. Make sure that you present the vision you have for your unit, company, or the entire organization, and know how to motivate others to pursue this vision. Make sure that others can see and feel the passion you experience in the workplace.

- Embracing decision-making. Develop the skills to make good decisions quickly while also considering the long-term effects of these actions. Be sure that your decisions reflect good judgment and decisiveness.

By actually implementing these strategies and working towards the development of their executive presence, leaders are granted success in their own environment and become some of others' best influencers.

In order to acquire resilience, leaders need to have a growth mindset and consider all setbacks and challenges as opportunities to learn either something new or improve current skills. Being capable of viewing problems as the instruments the leader can use to promote their skills and insight will help people continue to proceed easily. The other important attribute is adaptability as the circumstances can change within minutes and having the same principles regarding different situations is not the best approach for being a strong leader. There are some techniques that will assist in developing the qualities:

Self-care. To begin with, it will be beneficial to start taking care of oneself and monitor overall health. The factor is considered to be significant since people cannot achieve their objectives being overwhelmed by stress and unable to concentrate. Taking care of oneself in this context implies not only unlimited working hours but enough time for sleep and nutrition, sports activity, and communication with nature to extend the boundaries of the working world.

Strong support network. Another point is that every person, regardless of professional suitability, will not be able to make correct decisions all the time. However, a professional leader should have a strong support network that will be a ready help and make the right conclusions faster . For this purpose, people can encourage open communication with their team members and weekly group meetings to discuss recent cases and reactions.

Continuous learning. People should never stop learning something and should keep wondering and exploring something while evoking critical thinking. The best approach is to attend different workshops and conferences, read specific and professional literature, and employ modern technologies applicable to the new information.

When leaders actively cultivate their resilience and adaptability, they will thrive in times of uncertainty and change, while also demonstrating their leadership presence in an authentic way and inspiring others to do the same.

Leading With Integrity

One of the essential prerequisites for developing an influential leadership presence is to ensure that the leader is leading his or her team with integrity . When you are leading with integrity, you are not only establishing trust with your team members, but you are also fostering their loyalty and providing them with a positive work environment .

Demonstrate Ethical Decision-Making: in order to lead with integrity, you should ensure that you are making decisions that are in alignment with your system of values and ethical stances . Moreover, ethical decision making also requires to hold the needs of all stakeholders involved severely, as well as prioritizing the well-being of the organization first and foremost.

Embrace Transparency: being transparent means actively engaging your team members, providing them with clear information, and offering them timely updates regarding the status of each project . This type of leadership conduct should also be based on open communication that will create a significant sense of trust.

Practice Accountability: A another aspect of through which you can establish strong trust with your team followers is accountability . This implies holding yourself responsible for your actions and providing constructive feedback, yourself in the air excuse for any mistakes; in the meantime, you also encourage your followers to practice high levels of accountability in work by always keeping updated on the standard requirements and in the air expectance in a formal basis and making sure that they always proactively contribute to meeting team goals in the best possible way.

Foster Trust and Respect: On the final note, you may also implement policies that establish strong trust with your followers by incorporating certain measures that ensure consistently in your conduct and speech . Not only is respect for other people essential when you are in leadership position, but you should also actively listen to the views and needs of your team members and also create opportunities and a safe venue for dialogue.

By leading with integrity presence, you are also fostering a work environment in which people feel respected, motivated, and ready to actively engage in the creation of common goals. In addition, when you are sure that integrity is a common core of your leadership behavior, it will also help you increase your leadership presence and inspire others to establish this type of communication, as well.

Authentic Leadership Presence in Action

Finally, I believe that it is also incredibly important to familiarize yourself with real-life examples of authentic leadership presence, as in this way, you can only get inspiration from these stories, but you can also learn some lessons that you can apply in your leadership behavior.

The first example that comes to mind is a well-known entrepreneur and CEO of Microsoft, Satya Nadella. By focusing on empowering employees and adopting a culture of innovation, he has succeeded in making Microsoft one of the biggest technology companies in the world. Nadella's greatest achievements lie not in emphasizing growth and innovation, although these are equally important elements of his management module. Instead, it is his style of authentic leadership based on collaboration, empathy, and a growth mindset that have led to his success. Being empathetic and encouraging employees has not only made Microsoft a better place to work in, but it has also had an immediate impact on the organization's connections with customers and partners . One of the most salient key takeaways can be summarized as follows: leaders should always be open to alternative viewpoints and strive to nurture a creative culture in which employees always feel they are making a positive difference.

The second example is a well-known media personality and CEO of Harpo Productions, Oprah Winfrey. Unlike many other authentic leaders, Winfrey's authentic presence results directly from her role as a media personality; however, as both a TV host and a philanthropist, she continues to be effective in reaching millions of people to this day. Moreover, her personality deserves a closer look: she is as authentic and dedicated to her goals as a person can get. She constantly reiterates that she believes in the power of storytelling and insists that sharing personal experiences and learning from other people's stories is one of the most powerful tools in her arsenal. Therefore, if these lessons resonate with you and you would be willing to leverage their potential, I would recommend incorporating these lessons into your life.

Chapter Summary

Becoming an authentic leader is a process that involves reflecting on one's journey and taking action to grow and make an impact. It is possible to develop your leadership presence by using the tools and advice discussed in this chapter, and you can start by applying the concepts to your own leadership role. Review your journey and your experiences, highlighting the critical events that helped you shape your leadership values and style.

Understand your style and strengths, and be confident in your authentic self as a leader, as this will inspire people around you. In addition to this, practice continuously. Whenever you have a challenge or an opportunity to practice a concept discussed in this chapter, use it as an occasion to learn from experience and develop your authentic leadership presence. Finally, remember that this is not a one-time task, as leadership develops through action .

Allow yourself to grow and change as a leader as you move forward and evolve in your career. Use feedback to your advantage, as it is a useful tool to gain an understanding of how others perceive you and can help you learn from your developmental experiences, be open to new challenges and consider acquiring new skills to grow as a leader.

Chapter 15

Fostering a Culture of Innovation

In today's competitive business environment, what drives progress and success is innovation. By creating a culture that values creativity, collaboration and experimentation, you can fully unleash your team's potential to push the organization forward. Read on as we highlight some strategies of making an innovative work place and embracing the future possibilities.

Reasons for Innovation

Your organization requires innovation in order to succeed and grow; it is not just a buzzword. In today's world where everything is happening so fast competition has reached alarming levels forcing firms to embrace innovation in order to be relevant. We shall delve into why innovation matters and how it propels progress hence giving your company competitive advantage.

Stay ahead of the curve: Through innovations one can always stay ahead of his or her competitors in such markets that are ever changing. As you come up with new concepts daily, you will meet your customers' dynamic needs.

Drive efficiency and productivity: Innovation often leads to process improvements, allowing your organization to become more efficient and productive. Innovative thinking can help identify bottlenecks, streamline operations, and enhance overall performance.

Create differentiation: With innovation, you can differentiate your business from others in the industry. By developing unique products or offering innovative solutions, you can attract customers, build brand loyalty, and stand out in a crowded market.

Embrace disruption: Disruptive technologies are constantly emerging while traditional business models rapidly become obsolete because the world around us keeps changing. By adopting an innovative culture we enable ourselves to adapt to disruptions that come our way and leverage new opportunities as well as maneuvering through these shifts with flexibility.

Foster collaboration and creativity: This fosters collaboration among employees when they try out something different which is creative oriented for instance by setting value on new ideas as well as experimentation within teams this creates an environment where people feel free enough to think outside the box thus coming up with breakthrough solutions

Innovation does not take place at once but rather becomes a mentality that continues throughout. By putting innovation at the top of your list and ensuring it is important to every employee in an organization, you can create a future that will see your company progress, sustain talent and move towards new horizons.

Creating an Environment of Creativity

In order to encourage creativity and drive innovation, there is need for creating a suitable environment. Organizations can therefore unlock their full creative potential by implementing strategies that encourages coming up with new ideas, collaboration and experimentation mind-set.

Building a culture of creativity starts by setting the scene for inspiration. Here are some effective strategies to create an environment that nurtures innovation:

Promote open communication and encourage brainstorming sessions where employees feel comfortable sharing their ideas.

Provide dedicated spaces for collaboration, such as open-plan work areas or designated meeting rooms equipped with whiteboards and interactive technology.

Offer resources and tools that support creative thinking ,such as access to cutting-edge technology, subscriptions to relevant industry publications and online platforms, as well as having innovation labs.

Emphasize the importance of continuous learning and professional development, empowering employees to expand their knowledge and explore new areas of interest.

Encourage cross-pollination of ideas by facilitating interactions between different teams and departments so as to achieve multiple perspectives.

A supportive culture embracing experimentation also helps in fostering creativity. Encourage staffs to take calculated risks through learning from failures rather than shying away from innovation when there are setbacks.

By creating an environment that fosters creativity, organizations can effectively promote innovation and stay on the cutting edge of their industry.

The Role of Leadership in Encouraging Innovation

Leadership is at the forefront of fostering a culture of innovation in an organization. Good leaders not only motivate their teams, but also enable them to be more creative and innovative. They create an atmosphere where risk taking is encouraged, collaboration is promoted, and learning never ceases.

Developing Innovative Leaders: How?

Lead by example: This means that there should be accepting new ideas as well as calculated risks and seeking for opportunities to enhance growth.

Empower your employees: Provide freedom and resources needed by your team in order to discover innovative ideas and contribute differently.

Promote a Growth Mindset: Foster an environment where failures are seen as part of learning and development which drives willingness to experiment further.

Encourage Collaboration: To achieve this you must breakdowns silos between departments consisting different perspectives that can drive innovations in businesses.

Provide Support and Resources: Investment into training programs, tools, methodologies as well as other processes that can support creative thinking providing groundwork for experimentation which may result into breakthrough.

Inspiring a Culture of Innovation

Leadership sets the tone for how organizations create an environment conducive to innovation. When leaders make innovation a priority it gets encoded into the fabric of the organization empowering all employees at all levels to contribute to progress.

Through producing leaders who become advocates of creativity organizations will have an edge over others hence becoming competitive while fostering work cultures built around collaborative endeavors with groundbreaking ideas serving as key drivers for such enterprises survival on the market scene today.

Building a Diverse and Inclusive Culture

Diversity and inclusivity are essential when attempting to boost innovation. By having workforce that embraces every form diversity can take enhances invention. Bringing people from diverse backgrounds together provides opportunity for numerous insights that organizations can leverage upon creating abundance in terms of unique ideas coming up with knowledge based outcomes towards better decision making processes within any sphere or sector chosen.

An inclusive culture ultimately strengthens employee engagement, increases their satisfaction and builds an adaptive organization. Different talents, skills, experiences and knowledge collated from cultural diverse workforce brings about innovation.

Here are some ways organizations can foster diversity and inclusivity to promote innovation:

Embrace Diversity in Recruitment: Proactively seek candidates from various backgrounds including ethnicity, gender, age and abilities to tap into a wide range of skills and perspectives. Provide Training and Education: Create awareness within the organization through various diversity training programs thereby establishing an environment that is respectful and where everyone feels valued.

Promote Inclusive Leadership: Encourage leaders to be inclusive in their approach as well as encouraging employees to share ideas which they think are beneficial for the company. Good leadership plays an important role in enhancing inclusion and driving innovation.

Create Diverse Teams: This implies teams built with members from various backgrounds who have difference skills sets allowing synergy affecting innovative ideas exchange solving complex problems creatively.

Encourage Collaboration: Facilitate multi-disciplinary team interactions across all levels within the organization in order to provide an environment for exchange of ideas. Provide platforms for employees to air their views, make comments or suggestions that will enable them learn from each other.

To facilitate employee innovation, organizations must provide employees with resources and support. Organizations can tap into a wealth of diverse perspectives and ideas from within their workforce by giving employees autonomy alongside necessary resources and support.

Encouraging Risk-Taking and Learning from Failure

Failure acceptance is an important part of innovation, as it encourages risk-taking. Encouraging a culture that embraces risk-taking allows organizations to explore new frontiers and push boundaries. When individuals feel empowered to take calculated risks, they are more likely to think creatively and come up with groundbreaking ideas.

Innovation thrives when failures are viewed as valuable learning opportunities rather than sources of discouragement. By fostering an environment that accepts failure as the key to success, organisations can inspire their staff to think out of the box and try new things. Such an approach fuels a culture of perseverance, resilience, and continuous improvement.

What is the Significance of Creating Safe Spaces?

Creating safe spaces for risk taking requires providing confidence and support for employees who want to step outside their comfort zones. It needs an environment where mistakes are not penalized but rather looked upon as essential aspects leading towards invention. Once people feel secure enough to voice out their thoughts or make bold moves, they are likely going to contribute in full capacity creative wise.

Encouraging a Growth Mindset

Another step towards fostering an environment that supports risk taking is adopting a growth mindset. A growth mindset recognizes that abilities can be developed through dedication and hard work. By promoting the belief that failure is a natural part of the innovation process, organizations can create an environment that values resilience, adaptability, and perseverance.

Tips for Encouraging Risk-Taking and Learning from Failure

Lead by example: Leaders should demonstrate their willingness to take risks learning from failures effectively making them role models for other teams.

Provide clear guidelines: Having set boundaries will help people make informed choices based on past experiences.

Celebrate failures: An open conversation about failures and turning them into success should be cultivated in a company culture.

Encourage collaboration: Employees learn from each other's failures if they work together leading to innovation and mutual development.

Reward risk-taking: The culture of innovation is strengthened when those taking risks and learning from them are recognized.

In this present evolving world, by embracing risk-taking and failure as opportunities to learn, organizations will unlock their full innovative potential, thus achieving enduring success.

Empowering Employees to Innovate

Organizations that prioritize innovativeness have an edge over others particularly in today's rapidly changing business environment. One of the underlying catalysts for innovation is empowering employees to access their creative side and be part of the organization's innovative culture. By giving employees autonomy and providing them with the necessary resources and support, organizations can tap into the diverse perspectives and ideas within their workforce.

Fostering Autonomy

To give space for innovation among workers, there has to be self-governance. When employees have the freedom to explore new ideas and take ownership of their work, they are more likely to think outside the box and come up with innovative solutions. Encouraging autonomy also fosters a sense of ownership and accountability, motivating employees to take the initiative in driving innovation forward.

Providing Resources and Support

For innovation to thrive, it is necessary that along with autonomy, employees are given resources and support. It involves access to the right tools, technologies and training that can improve their skills and competencies. Organizations can let the employees develop by investing in them these organizations allow them to think outside the box and support the goal of innovation.

Supportive Environment

Apart from autonomy and resources, a supportive environment is important for enabling employees to be more innovative. This includes creating conditions that promote experiments; appreciating different perspectives; as well as encouraging collaboration. Therefore, through allowing staff to take risks while sharing new ideas in safe environment, companies can tap into full potential of their human resources.

Recognition and Rewarding Innovation

Finally, sustaining an empowering culture of innovation requires recognition of innovative efforts. Not only does this motivate individuals, but also sets good examples for other people too. Thus organizations may choose to integrate recognition and rewards into performance appraisal processes so as to further promote creativity among workers hence driving innovation.

In conclusion, employee empowerment for innovativeness is an essential ingredient of creating a culture of innovation within organizations. Autonomous decision-making processes; providing necessary resources; having supportive environments; recognizing innovations are some ways in which companies can tap into creative power of their personnel and achieve sustainable growth over time.

Cross-Functional Collaboration

Company success hinges on collaborative relationships for its innovation. Companies should encourage cross-functional team work by removing barriers between departments or units to unlock team potentials thereby achieving breakthrough innovations.

When different teams and departments work together towards common goals, diverse perspectives meet expertise leading to generation of new ideas and creative solutions. Collaborative environments foster a sense of shared ownership and accountability thus nurturing an innovative-friendly culture.

Breaking Silos for Innovation

Eliminate obstacles that hinder collaboration across teams or departments through open communication channels for information exchange.

Facilitate regular cross-functional meetings and brainstorming sessions aimed at knowledge sharing, idea generation & collaboration.

Create avenues for continued collaboration, such as digital platforms, where workers can cooperate on projects and provide updates in real-time.

Benefits of Cross-Functional Collaboration

Enhanced problem-solving: Such teams bring together people with diverse skills and perspectives to deal with complex problems.

Innovative thinking: Teamwork prompts innovative thinking since members offer new insights and different ways of tackling issues.

Efficiency and speed: Minimizing duplication of efforts through breaking silos results into effectiveness that assists organizations to respond quickly to markets' demands.

Improved decision-making: It enables better-informed decisions by bringing together a variety of expertise for cross-functional collaboration.

Fostering an environment of cross-functional collaboration leads to an ecosystem where innovation flourishes. By breaking down silos and promoting collaborative innovation, ideas are transformed, improvements are made and growth becomes sustainable.

Embracing a Continuous Improvement Mindset

To promote innovation and stay ahead in today's fast-paced, ever-changing business landscape, it is important for firms to embrace a culture of continuous improvement. This can foster innovation and enable organizations to adapt their products, processes or services based on the changing needs of their target customers through continuously improving them.

Creating a culture that values continuous improvement involves:

Encouraging a Learning Culture: Create an atmosphere where employees are inspired to keep learning and developing themselves. This may include training opportunities for workshops and knowledge exchange which will help them grow up.

Enthusiasm for Iteration: Teams should be motivated to use an iterative approach and then assess and improve their work on a regular basis. This allows them to generate new ideas and fine-tune their solutions through incremental improvement.

Creating a Feedback Loop: Design people policies that encourage frank, open and constructive feedback within the organization. Employees need to participate by sharing their thoughts, speeches as well as suggestions to facilitate insights that can drive continuous improvements.

In addition, businesses can take advantage of technology and data to continuously improve. They can also identify gaps for further enhancement, make data driven decisions and evaluate the effectiveness of such initiatives using analytics paired with performance metrics.

The embracing of continuous improvement mindset enables organizations to create an environment where learning is valued while fostering innovation. It not only helps them to remain competitive in today's ever changing business world but also makes them capable of exploiting emerging markets so as to enhance long term efficiency.

The Art of Measuring Innovation

Organizations must measure innovation if they wish to develop it further and stay ahead in the competition. Companies can get insights into their innovative processes, find out what went wrong or which direction they should take through effective measurement techniques. For instance, one way is by having key performance indicators (KPIs) on innovation alone like number of new product line releases or patents filed or cost savings from process innovations. Surveys are another method that may be used by companies among other mechanisms including surveys where employees and stakeholders are asked questions about how they perceive innovation within firms. The comments offered will provide management with holistic perspective on how innovation culture is practiced hence helping it understand its strengths and weaknesses.

Equally important is recognizing the effort put forth into innovating in order to motivate individuals as well as teams behind driving this change forward. Where employees' efforts towards being innovative are appreciated it creates an atmosphere that supports its culture; thus more people will think differently about things. Recognition could involve giving awards to staff members who have shown the most innovation, displaying innovative products or even having special areas in the workplace that are dedicated to showcasing successful breakthrough projects.

Through combining meaningful recognition with effective measurement, companies can create a working environment that encourages and appreciates innovations. This creates positive feedback loops that lead to continuous improvements as well as sustaining innovations resulting in shaping the company's DNA hence positioning it for success.

Chapter 16

Performance Management and Motivation

Performance management is the provision of goal setting, on going feedback, and evaluating the overall performance of the team or the organization. Motivation is the factor or factors that drive or impel an individual to succeed and do well and to be committed to the end result. Knowing a few simple theories of both will help a leader create a motivated productive team. Performance management is a simple, logical process; people who do not have goals are almost certainly not going to achieve them. Set goals, either with or for the employee, let him or her know why those goals are being set and the process and timetable for evaluation, and then periodically check on work progress and consult with the employee on performance related issues.

This employee then, will be more concerned with his or her own growth, more oriented to the growth of the organization and in terms of their skills expose to their career of their interest. Thus, employees will take personal responsibility for their progress and actions. Through flexibility, communication and structure, the organization secures invaluable return on its investment.

Principles and Benefits of Performance Management

Performance management is a process through which organizations can ensure that their employees' work is of the highest quality and provided the greatest benefits. By understanding the principles which guide this technique, businesses and private companies can structure it in such a way that it can increase motivation, align employees' interests with those of their employer, and help maintain a clear focus on specific objectives. An ideal way of beginning the study of any such process is examining the reasons for maintaining goals, as this ability underlies all of the other goals of management. Let us take show the reasons why one must work with targets and describe the ideal way to use them.

Intensity and Will. When individuals work toward explicitly defined goals, they are more willing to apply themselves and work with greater intensity. This results in them achieving better results in similar fields in which those without targets produce poor results.

Clarity of Goals. When employees have clear goals they can pursue, the can tell what their interests are. This results in them being more likely to protect these interests if they are in any way threatened.

Reviewing Goals. In cases where individuals have clearly defined objectives and goals, they can periodically review their performance and work out if they are close to achieving these targets.

Generation of Motivation. Setting people clear goals ensures that their desire to achieve them can act as a source of motivation, allowing them to push harder than would be typical.

One of the most important skills that a senior manager can develop and teach their employees is the ability to work with goals and targets. This can best be done by helping the employees plan and structure the goals they choose to establish into those which are Specific, Measurable, Achievable, Relevant, and Time-bound. Finally, one should actively engage their employees in the process of goal-setting so that these objectives could best take into account their interests and opportunities.

1. Regular check-ins – provide ongoing support and feedback throughout the goal setting journey. Regular check-ins help to monitor progress and make appropriate adjustments.
2. Celebrate milestones – after an employee has achieved a certain milestone, celebrate it. This helps to boost their morale and continuing motivation. Therefore, by setting clear goals and providing the proper support, a manager can enable other employees to perform excellently and contribute to the success of the organization.

Topic 5: Providing Feedback for Growth

Feedback is a crucial element of performance as it helps individuals work towards their best potential. Effective feedback provides insights into an individual's progress, reinforces positive behavior, and identifies areas to develop. This topic provides information on the importance of feedback, types or models of feedback, and how to provide feedback.

The Importance of Feedback

Feedback is an important element of performance as it drives learning, development, and continuous improvement. With feedback, managers and leaders can:

- Highlight an employee's strengths and successes. This in turn boosts their motivation to continue performing excellently.
- Identify areas that the employee needs to improve or develop and actively challenge the employee to do so.
- Set the right expectations and align an employee's goals with the organization's goals.
- Emphasize good behavior, open communication, and trust among employees and their managers. This in turn will help to improve their professional relationships with others.

Different Feedback Models

To help provide the right feedback, different feedback models have been developed. Two common examples that are used to provide constructive feedback to employees include:

- The sandwich model , which starts with positive feedback, goes through feedback and the areas that need to improve, and finishes up with another positive comment.
- The GROW model focuses on Goal, Reality, Options, and Will. Managers and other employees need to identify an individual's goals, analyze what the current situation is , identify what other options are available, and then assess whether the employee is willing to take action .
- Be specific and objective – give clear examples and focus on specific behaviors or actions, not generalizations.
- Focus on behavior, not the individual – separate performance criticisms from personal attacks to avoid putting the person receiving feedback on the defensive and cultivate a growth mindset.
- Deliver feedback in a timely manner – give feedback as close as possible to when the behavior was observed to ensure it is relevant and impactful.
- Use active listening – give the team member the chance to respond and actively listen to their feedback or concerns.
- Offer solutions and support – provide guidance, resources, and help to improve performance and address challenges.
- Encourage a feedback culture – create a work environment where open and honest feedback is welcomed, valued, and seen as an opportunity for growth. Based on this knowledge, feedback models, and delivery strategies, managers can

ensure employees are in an environment that allows them to keep learning and developing and stay engaged at work.

Assessment and Evaluation of Performance

Performance assessments and evaluations are critical to any organization's strategic plans. They help understand if employees are efficient in their roles. Furthermore, they promote a culture of learning and improvement . In this respect, different evaluation techniques can be used.

Performance appraisals – " performance appraisals are a simple evaluation method that requires supervisors to review an employee's prior accomplishments, credentials, and vision for the future ". Performance appraisals allow organizations to set clear expectations for employees based on established benchmarks. Therefore, employees can be informed of how their work can contribute to the organization's mission.

360-Degree feedback – "this type of evaluation involves data collection from multiple personnel ". This data can be collected from managers, peers, subordinates, clients, and vendors. It allows for assessing the quality of relationships formed by an employee within the organization.

Performance Metrics

Performance metrics, such as key performance indicators , provide organizations with numerical data to evaluate performance. By tracking specific data points, such as sales targets, customer satisfaction scores, or productivity levels, organizations can objectively assess an employee's performance and note any areas of concern. .

Leveraging Multiple Methods

Organizations can utilize a combination of different assessment methods to get a more holistic view of performance. By utilizing both performance appraisals and 360-degree feedback, organications can leverage data from multiple sources . For example, an organization can use performance appraisals to focus on an employee's overall performance and estimate their potential for promotion . They can also combine this data with 360-degree feedback to know the employee's performance from third-party stakeholders and compare it with the appraisdal data. Also, organizations can then leverage both data to assess an employee's performance and potential and get a bigger picture.

When assessing performance, it is important to not just focus on the employee's shortcomings, but also focus on identifying their strengths. By identifying the areas where the employee is performing well, organizations can provide a more balanced and fair assessment. This approach can facilitate growth and development by recording the employee's strengths and leveraging them for growth. Ultimately, organizations can use these assessments to enhance their employees' performance and productivity.

Motivating Employees for High Performance.

Motivation is an important factor in driving high performance. When an individual is motivated, they are more engaged, productive, and committed to reaching their goals. As a manager, you should understand how different motivation theories and techniques work. In this essay, I will present some practical strategies for motivating employees to reach high performance. They are as follows:

- Set Clear Expectations. Communicate your expectations and define your specific performance goals . If employees understand what you expect from them, it can motivate them to achieve high performance.

Meaningful work

Employees work when you assign challenging and meaningful tasks that exploit their talents and values. If workers see their work as meaningful and interesting, they will be further motivated to do their best. One way of ascribing meaning to their work is through offering an inspiring vision of where they are heading. This will serve as a powerful weapon for improving motivation and working towards achieving a shared goal.

Recognition and rewards

Recognition and rewards work. A simple "Thank you" would work wonders, if employees understand that it is sincere. Financial rewards are even more effective for making employees feel valued and important. People spend time, knowledge and even health for the company's cause, and they want to be recognized and appreciated for that. The most appropriate form of recognition is the one that is expected and wanted by the employee receiving it.

Growth and development

As an employer, you need to provide opportunities for growth and development since improving employee motivation is largely dependent on employees learning and growing. Thus, organizations should hire employees capable of learning and commit their time and resources to the same employees. The best source of motivation is the one that comes from within.

Relationship

Improvement of motivation in an organization can be achieved through nurturing a culture of relationship both between employees and employer and between employees. People appreciate being part of a team, of being in a choir where they are able to harmonize with the rest. People need to support one another, rather than be competitors. A lot of people get displaced and downsized nowadays because every company is interested in its strategies and results instead of the people.

The following are recommendations for the development of recognition and reward practices:

- Provide personalized rewards . Different employees possess different preferences and motivators. Thus, it is necessary to provide them with individualized rewards associated with their interests and goals. These can be bonuses, rewards, gift cards, extra time-off, or even a chance to be developed as a specialist.
- Implement peer-to-peer recognition system. In such a way, employees will feel the support and appreciate each other's work. Therefore, they will feel safer and encourage the creation of a supporting work environment.
- Reward employees with opportunities for growth. Apart from tangible rewards, employees need to receive opportunities for developing their careers and expanding roles in the same organization. Reward performance with challenges or initiate a mentorship program from long-time company leaders. Alternatively, invite the recognition program to sponsor their subordinate in one of the professional development or relevant courses.
- Periodically review and change your recognition program. It is necessary to review it to make sure its bringing up positive results. Receives managers' reflection and employees" feedback, make sure to ask them about proposed changes or additions. Make regular comments and act on feedback collected to improve existing practices.

The promotion of such recognitions and reward practices will trigger positive changes in the work environment. Let's not forget that willing employees will require the creation of a pleasant atmosphere and the possibility of further recognition. In such a way, managers can be sure that their employees will be willing to work beyond their expectations.

Building a Performance Management Culture

Building a culture of performance management is very critical as such enables the organization to be able to maintain very high levels of motivation and productivity. By aligning the goals and expectations of the employees with the overall competency and capacity of the organization, it is possible to enhance the performance of individuals and teams.

If the organization wants to have a performance-driven culture, there are certain strategies it should apply, including:

- communication, making the company's mission, vision, and the goals clearly understood to the entire staff will give employees a sense of purpose and belonging;
- goal alignment, encouraging the alignment of employees' personal goals with those of an organization will motivate them to perform at the best of their ability in order to contribute to the company's betterment;

- regular performance reviews, these should be conducted often so that there is a chance to assess employee's progress and give a response where some gaps occur with a goal to improve subsequent performances ;
- training and development, employees should be supported in their efforts to learn and better themselves, and they should be given a chance to acquire necessary skills and knowledge;
- recognizing and rewarding, the rewards and recognition system should be fair and substantial so that the best performing employees are encouraged to keep up the good work and the underachievers are motivated to improve;
- support and involvement of leaders, it is the leadership that sets the tone for any company which is prepared to have performance-driven culture and their managers had to lead by example .

All of these examples together can create a system within a framework of which good practice can operate. In such an environment, employees are more engaged, motivated, and satisfied. Psychological contract is strengthened, and business prospects are generally much more optimistic than those facing organization without any such strategies in place.

Challenges in Performance Management and Motivation and How to Overcome Them

Though implementation of performance management and motivation is highly beneficial for the organizations and their employees, various challenges may be faced. It is rather significant for organizations to understand and overcome such challenges as lack of clear communication and goal alignment, resistance to change, and sustaining motivation.

The first challenge is associated with the lack of clear communication and goal alignment. It is critical for employees to understand what is expected from them and how their effort contributes to the overall goal of the organization . Organizations should ensure that their goals are effectively communicated to the employees and should establish transparent setting of these goals . Employees should understand the goals of the organization as well as how they contribute to the achievement of these goals.

Resistance to change is another significant challenge. There may be employees who have never seen performance management and motivation practices in use. Also, some employees may be skeptical toward such approaches. To overcome these challenges the organizations should ensure that the employees understand the positive consequences of implementation of performance management and motivation for their personal growth, career development, and job satisfaction . Training and support to managers and employees may also be rather effective to help employees to adjust to new practices.

Sustaining motivation over time may also be a critical issue as though some approaches may significantly increase the employee motivation initially, but the constant sustainability of motivation is required . For sustainability of motivation the organizations need to evaluate regularly the changes of employees' needs and modify the motivational practices accordingly . Outstanding performance should be recognized and rewarded regularly, and a positive work culture should be promoted where every employee feels the value of their contribution.

Chapter 17

Crisis Management and Resilience

In this chapter, we are going to talk about crisis management and resilience. In the fast-paced and highly competitive business industry today, companies are presented with unforeseen events that may threaten their stability and success. It is important for organizations to have a planned response to these events so they can bounce back stronger than ever.

What is Crisis Management?

Crisis management involves various strategies that aim to mitigate damage during crises. These crises could range from natural disasters, financial issues, security breaches, reputational harm, etc. The importance of effective crisis management cannot be overstated as it allows companies to maintain operational resilience and reduce impact.

One aspect of crisis management is preparedness through proper planning. This means identifying potential problems within the organization early on and developing strategies to address them. By doing this, companies will be more well-equipped in handling unexpected situations.

Another component of crisis management is putting together a comprehensive crisis response plan. This plan outlines the steps that should be taken once a crisis hits. Procedures and communication protocols are also included in this document along with assigned roles and responsibilities for stakeholders involved in resolution.

To effectively manage a crisis, organizations must establish strong communication channels as well. By being transparent with stakeholders at times like these (employees, customers, general public), companies can maintain trust while minimizing damage brought about by the crisis event.

Building organizational resilience should also be prioritized by businesses aiming for long-term stability. This involves adopting innovative practices and strategies which will allow the company to bounce back stronger after challenges have been faced.

Lastly, learning from past crises is crucial for continuous improvement. Lessons learned from real-life examples will enhance your company's future problem-solving capabilities while keeping up with dynamic corporate environments.

Knowing what you're dealing with

Every business faces different challenges that may escalate into full-blown crises if not addressed properly at an early stage. To prevent such escalation from happening within your organization, you must proactively identify potential triggers and address them immediately.

Conducting a thorough assessment of your company's operations, internal processes, and external environment would be a great start in identifying these triggers. This allows you to uncover vulnerabilities that you may be blind to and anticipate potential crises that may come your way.

Here are some steps to help you identify potential crisis triggers:

Data Analytics: Use tools and processes that deal with data analytics to see if you can identify patterns, trends, and potential risks. You need to know if anything could trigger a crisis. To do this, analyze both quantitative and qualitative data so that you can learn about your organization's weak points and what parts should be concerning for you.

Risk Assessment: This step requires a thorough risk assessment in order to figure out which threats are on the horizon threatening a crisis. Rate each of these risks based off of how likely they are to happen as well as the impact they'll have on your business.

Internal Audits: Regularly take time out to do internal audits in order for you to figure out whether or not your systems and processes (and controls) are effective at doing their job. If it isn't successful at doing its job then you need to go back go square one until it is ready.

External Monitoring: Keep an eye makes sure you keep an eye on all aspects surrounding your industry, competitors, and business landscape. Monitor market trends, regulatory changes, etc., etc., so that ultimately when something poses potential challenges or opportunities you will know right away.

Employee Engagement: It sounds basic but simply encourage employees to report any signs of concern or issues that they see. Also make sure that there is a way for them to do this (feedback loop). When feedback comes through make sure there is someone who will listen right away!

Create a Crisis Communication Plan: Develop an elaborate plan outlining communication procedures, messaging strategies, and spokesperson roles. Regularly update this plan and make it easily accessible to all relevant stakeholders.

Be Transparent and Authentic: Share information openly. Admit the difficulty of the situation and provide honest updates. Being transparent and authentic builds trust with stakeholders.

Utilize Multiple Communication Channels: Reach out to stakeholders through various channels. Social media, press releases, website updates, and direct communication have different audiences that need to be reached.

Prepare Key Messages: Develop clear messages that address the crisis, its impact, and the organization's response in a way that is easily understood by everyone involved.

Monitor and Respond to Feedback: Keep a close eye on your communication channels for feedback. Address any concerns quickly. Engage in open dialogue with stakeholders showing them you are willing to listen and adjust as needed.

By implementing these crisis communication strategies, organizations can effectively manage corporate challenges while maintaining transparency, credibility, and stakeholder trust.

Building Organizational Resilience

Building organizational resilience is crucial for navigating today's dynamic corporate landscape. By doing so businesses can overcome the many challenges they face by bouncing back stronger from crises making them more adaptable and agile entities

Here are some strategies that companies can adopt to strengthen their organizational resilience:

Developing a Growth Mindset: Encouraging employees to embrace a growth mindset fosters a culture of continuous learning and improvement. Challenges will be viewed as opportunities for growth allowing companies to adapt more effectively.

Diversify Operations & Manage Risk: Diversifying operations helps mitigate unexpected challenge impacts. When you identify risk beforehand it allows you to navigate crises more effectively while minimizing potential disruptions.

Invest in Employee Well-being: Prioritizing employee well-being boosts morale which boosts their resilience levels as well. Provide them with support systems like training resources so they can better handle difficult situations when they arise.

Establish Effective Crisis Systems : Implementing effective crisis management systems enhances an organizations ability to respond swiftly and effectively to crises. Regularly updating these systems ensures they remain adaptable and aligned with evolving corporate challenges.

Build Strong Partnerships: Collaboration is key, especially when it comes to external partners, suppliers, and stakeholders. Having strong relationships can help organizations access additional resources so they can fight through the tough times.

By embracing these strategies and practices companies can build their organizational resilience which will enable them to withstand and recover from crises with greater effectiveness. In doing so, they position themselves for long-term success in an increasingly volatile business environment.

Testing and Evaluating Crisis Preparedness

In today's rapidly evolving business landscape organizations need to be prepared at all times. Regularly testing crisis preparedness is a great way to ensure that you are up to date with your crisis management technique.

Methods for Testing Crisis Preparedness

Simulation exercises: These exercises allow organizations to test their response plans in a controlled environment. Through this simulation you'll be able to identify gaps, refine processes, and improve overall preparedness.

Tabletop exercises: Tabletop exercises involve discussions and role-playing. These simulate crisis situations allowing you to evaluate decision-making processes, communication flow, and coordination among key stakeholders.

Scenario Analysis: By examining the past and proposing hypothetical situations, organizations are able to gauge how prepared they are for future events. This allows them to address flaws in their system and create a more efficient response strategy.

The Importance of Evaluation

Regularly assessing your ability to handle crises is necessary for growth. It allows you to see what areas need improving, what needs to be changed, and what lessons can be learned from real world examples.

Key Areas for Evaluation

Response time: Gauge how quickly you were able to identify a crisis and begin responding. How fast did you escalate it? Are there any glaringly slow parts of your process that need changing?

Communication effectiveness: Evaluate how well information is presented during a crisis. Identify where clarity was lost or unnecessary secrecy was given.

Coordination and collaboration: Assess the efficiency of working with both internal departments and external partners. Were there any noticeable complications that could be improved?

Through these evaluations, companies can locate vulnerabilities in their defense system, plug holes, and improve their abilities so they're ready for whatever corporate challenges come their way.

Learning from Past Crises

By digging into real-world scenarios, organizations can learn from past mistakes and enhance their management capabilities moving forward. Post-mortem analyses allow businesses to pinpoint what specifically caused previous failures as well as understand what red flags were missed or ignored.

Identify the key factors that led to the crisis.

Analyze the organization's response and effectiveness in managing the crisis.

Evaluate the outcomes and consequences of the crisis.

Upon finishing these post-mortem analyses companies will have a thorough understanding of what went wrong in their previous approach. By addressing these negatives directly they'll develop better habits for handling future issues.

Moreover, studying successful stories provides valuable insight into navigating emergencies effectively. Analyzing how other organizations overcame obstacles gives businesses inspiration for their own techniques as well as ideas on how they could improve further down the line. These case studies serve as valuable sources of knowledge and inspiration to support organizations in building resilience and mitigating future crises.

Throughout this process it is pivotal that businesses incorporate these lessons into their crisis management plans. By continuing their education on the subject and regularly updating their strategies they'll remain up to date and well equipped for anything that comes their way.

Implementing Continuous Improvement Strategies

As companies navigate through corporate challenges, continuous improvement becomes increasingly important. This mindset allows them to embrace solutions head on, better themselves, and achieve resiliency. Through constant refinement organizations can proactively address vulnerabilities in their system, enhance their crisis management capabilities, and minimize potential damages.

Adaptability is a crucial part of the improvement process. When businesses stay nimble and can go with the flow, they'll be able to navigate any crisis before it can take hold. This means frequently evaluating all existing processes, systems, and protocols, looking for necessary changes that will help as different corporate challenges arise. As cliché as it sounds, embracing change and staying ahead is essential in today's wild world.

Agility isn't just a buzzword — it's a key tool in a successful crisis management toolbox. Companies that can quickly pivot away from their current strategies are much more prepared to withstand unforeseen events. A solid plan should always have provisions for flexibility and rapid decision-making. That way organizations can respond promptly to new threats.

And finally, innovation plays perhaps the most important role in all this. By constantly pushing employees to come up with new ideas and think outside the box, companies will find themselves better equipped to handle anything that comes their way. They need to be ready to jump on emerging technologies without hesitation (or skepticism), use analytics responsibly but often, and adopt proven best practices when appropriate. If you don't innovate now, you won't survive later!

Chapter 18

Ethical and
Values-Based Leadership

In this section, we will explore the principles of ethical and values-based leadership and delve into the importance of integrity and responsible governance in today's leaders.

As leade-rs, it is extremely important to compre-hend the importance of principle-d leadership and its effe-ct on organizations and society altogether. By pe-rsonifying robust values and furthering accountable de-cision making, leaders can make optimistic change-and nourish a climate of trustworthiness and honesty.

Throughout this section, we- will look at different parts of moral manageme-nt, including the part of sincerity, the significance- of choices depend on qualitie-s, and the transformative intensity of ge-nuine administration. We will likewise- investigate how passionate insight plays a basic part in moral choice- making forms and how moral initiative can shape associations in a worldwide se-tting. Furthermore-, strategies will be e-xamined for cultivating principled leade-rs and nurturing an organizational culture grounded in ethics, with spe-cial focus on the part of leadership advance-ment programs in cultivating the fundamental qualitie-s expected of principle-d leadership.

In closing, we- will gaze towards tomorrow, investigating deve-loping patterns and practices in moral and principles-base-d guidance. By keeping notifie-d about these patterns, le-aders can change and lead the-ir organizations in an ever-evolving world, confirming accountable-administration and upright behavior.

Le-t us begin this adventure of principle-d and values-centere-d leadership, where- honesty, accountability, and a dedication to moral behavior form the- foundation of our leadership methods. If we- work as a team, we can craft a brighter tomorrow for companie-s and motivate others to guide with inte-ntion and ethics top of mind. We all wish to do good while doing we-ll. With care and cooperation, our visions can uplift people- and bring out their best.

Understanding Ethical Leadership

In today's constantly shifting commercial e-nvironment defined by intricacy, principle-d leadership arises as a guiding light for e-nterprises see-king sustained achieveme-nt. At its core, principled leade-rship champions virtue, principles and accountable de-cision making. By embracing these fundame-ntals, leaders construct a basis of trustworthiness, cle-arness and genuinene-ss within their organisations.

Leade-rship with integrity considers more than just rule-s. It means choosing options that match moral principles and encouraging an e-nvironment where pe-ople act rightly. Staying true to what you belie-ve is extreme-ly important for leaders, espe-cially when choices are tough.

Values also play an indispe-nsable role in principled le-adership. A leader's principle-s mold their behavior and stee-r their decision-making processe-s, impacting the overall organizational culture. By e-mbracing and exhibiting principles such as impartiality, truthfulness, and re-sponsibility, leaders motivate the-ir teams to act ethically and uphold high standards.

What is Ethical Leadership?

Honesty and trust: Ethical leadership is based on honesty, consistency and trustworthiness. Leaders who are transparent in their actions and communication create an open and accountable environment. Core values: A leader's values act as a guide, directing decisions and setting the tone for the whole organization. By acting according to values like respect, fairness and empathy, leaders develop an ethical culture throughout the organization.

Thoughtful decisions: Ethical leaders consider carefully how decisions may affect others. They prioritize ethics over personal gain, aiming to choose options that reflect fairness, social responsibility and long-term sustainability.

By adopting principles of e-thical leadership, companies can nurture- an environment of trustworthiness, re-sponsibility, and sound management. This approach simultaneously stre-ngthens a firm's reputation while re-cruiting and keeping exce-llent employee-s who appreciate principled de-cisions and leadership guided by moral standards.

The Importance of Values-Based Leadership

Values-base-d leadership is a key part of making e-thical choices within companies. It includes core- ideals and beliefs that guide- how leaders act. When manage-rs base choices on a company's important principles, the-y support good conduct and build a workplace where pe-ople have integrity and re-ly on each other.

Values-base-d leadership looks beyond just obe-ying policies and procedures; it include-s moral reflections and advances the- overall well-being. It inspire-s leaders to make choice-s grounded in mutual principles like truthfulne-ss, regard, impartiality, and social accountability.

Key Benefits of Values-Based Leadership:

Be-tter Ethical Decision Making: Leade-rship focused on values allows leade-rs to navigate complex moral issues by sticking to cle-ar guiding principles. This ensures choice-s align with the company's standards of right and wrong, made with eve-ryone's best intere-sts in mind.

Positive Company Atmosphere: Le-aders demonstrating values-guide-d leadership set the-tone for the whole organization. Staff more- readily trust and respect le-aders prioritizing ethics, leading to a ple-asant work environment and higher job satisfaction.

Stronge-r Relationships with Intereste-d Parties: Prioritizing values-guided le-adership, leaders build de-ep authentic connections with inte-rested parties like- customers, suppliers, and the community. The-se relationships founded on trust, re-liability and mutual respect. Long-Term Achie-vement: Companies e-mbracing values-guided leade-rship tend to have bette-r long-term success and sustainability. By making decisions first conside-ring ethical issues, leade-rs establish a strong basis for the organization's future growth and progre-ss.

Overall, prioritizing e-thical values helps drive de-cision-making rooted in integrity within companies. By cultivating a culture- that respects people- and principles, leaders can e-stablish a constructive setting where- high standards of conduct are maintained, trust is cultivated, and long-te-rm achievement is accomplishe-d.

Building Trust Through Authentic Leadership

Authentic le-adership creates a trusting e-nvironment and positive work culture. Le-aders who act naturally encourage ope-nness. Teams fee-l safe sharing ideas and working togethe-r.

Information flows freely betwe-en different parts of the- company. Here are key ways in which authentic leadership promotes trust-building:

Leading by Personal Example: Genuine leaders guide with honesty and stay true to their beliefs. By consistently demonstrating ethical behavior and making decisions that align with their principles, they gain the trust and respect of their team.

Open and Straightforward Communication: Authentic leaders prioritize clear and transparent communication. They actively listen to their team's ideas, concerns, and feedback, creating a safe space where all feel valued and heard.

Building Meaningful Relationships: Genuine leaders invest in developing caring relationships with their team. By showing care and empathy, they establish a sense of trust and create a supportive environment where people can thrive.

Encouraging Teamwork: Authentic leaders foster a collaborative culture where everyone's contributions are valued. By promoting working together, they empower their team to share ideas, collaborate, and make use of their combined strengths.

Authentic le-adership cultivates belie-f within groups and additionally adds to the general prospe-rity and execution of an association. When group individuals trust the-ir pioneers, they fe-el energize-d, included, and are bound to exte-nd themselves in the-ir work.

Promoting ethical conduct and transpare-ncy within an organization is crucial as it reinforces the principle-s of trustworthiness and integrity. When a company ope-rates with openness and hone-sty, prioritizing fair treatment of all people-, it establishes reliability and confide-nce among employee-s as well as customers. Such values lay the- groundwork for mutual understanding and respect be-tween an organization and the community it se-rves. Upholding high standards of behavior helps stre-ngthen relationships and fosters coope-ration

Promoting Ethical Conduct and Transparency

Creating a positive- work environment built to last starts with encouraging e-thical behavior and openness. By making the-se priorities, companies can de-velop a culture based on trust, re-sponsibility and honesty. When employe-es feel the-y work for an organization dedicated to doing the right thing, it le-ads to successful collaboration and productivity. Leaders who communicate- clear standards of conduct and allow transparency reinforce- the shared goal of mee-ting challenges with respe-ct, care and fairness.

Ethical conduct is e-ssential, as it establishes how pe-ople within a company communicate and make choice-s. Aligning behavior with moral standards guarantees e-quity and fairness in all parts of operations. When companie-s encourage ethics, worke-rs feel motivated to be- truthful and keep noble principle-s. Integrity and respect form the- basis of relationships inside an organization and with outside partie-s. Prioritizing right over wrong helps build trust with eve-ryone the business inte-racts with.

Being ope-n goes together with moral be-havior, as it includes clear communication and sharing all details. Whe-n groups share openly about what they do, choose-, and how they work, they gain trust betwe-en workers, customers, and those- involved. Openness make-s a feeling of honesty and de-creases the chance-s of bad behavior happening without being se-en.

Benefits of promoting ethical conduct and transparency:

To instill ethical conduct and transpare-ncy, companies can develop unambiguous e-thical principles and values, provide consiste-nt ethics instruction, and nurture an environme-nt of straightforward communication and criticism. Leaders play a pivotal function in modeling the-se values and upholding them, ge-nerating a cascading impact throughout the organization.

 Ultimately, whe-n companies make ethics and ope-nness a priority, they build a positive workplace- where people- can excel and rely on e-ach other. This results in bette-r work, happier customers, and long-lasting achieve-ment.

Ethical Leadership in Decision-Making

Leade-rs frequently deal with difficult situations that re-quire making ethical choices. The-se choices nee-d careful thought and following ethical guideline-s. The decision making process involve-s working through moral problems and making sure any choices match the-organization's values of right and wrong.

Identifying and unde-rstanding complex ethical situations can be challe-nging. These situations eme-rge when decision-make-rs face circumstances involving competing principle-s and important values. Assessing how choices may affe-ct interested partie-s and weighing the outcomes of e-ach option requires considering the- perspectives of othe-rs.

Navigating Moral Dilemmas

To thoughtfully handle complicate-d situations, people in charge can gain from care-fully **Considering choices through these steps:** Clearly defining the dile-ma. Make sure eve-ryone agrees on spe-cifically what issues need addre-ssing .Identifying the affected partie-s. Recognizing the moral concerns involved. Collecting applicable data and thinking about different viewpoints. Using ethical models and standards to examine the circumstance. Investigating other solutions and assessing their possible outcomes. Making a well-thought decision based on moral benchmarks and principles

By systematically conside-ring the ethical implications of decisions, le-aders can reduce the-chance of choices that undermine- moral principles. A thoughtful examination allows important values to guide- complex situations, rather than being an afte-rthought. With care and wisdom, a fair outcome respe-cting all people can be found.

Utilizing Ethical Frameworks

An e-thical structure offers directors a group of rule-s or concepts that can help guide the-ir choice making procedures. The-se structures assist directors asse-ss the virtue of their activitie-s and guarantee respe-ctable conduct. Moral standards give chiefs a compass to all the- more likely settle- on choices that think about how their choices will affe-ct others. They cente-r around acting with trustworthiness, regard, responsibility and compassion. An e-thical system encourages leaders to settle on choices that benefit their team and society as a whole.

There are several widely recognized ethical frameworks, including:

Utilitarianism focuses on bringing the- most happiness to the greate-st number of people. It aims to maximize- overall welfare.

De-ontological ethics emphasizes following a se-t of moral rules and duties that apply to all people-. It focuses on adherence- to universal principles.

Virtue e-thics focuses on developing good characte-r and moral values. It emphasizes cultivating virtuous pe-rsonality traits. Justice ethics emphasize-s fairness and ensuring outcomes are- equitable for eve-ryone. It focuses on bringing just and fair outcomes for all.

Leade-rs can utilize these frame-works as guides to steer the-ir decision-making process and assess the- moral consequences of the-ir choices. By recognizing the- challenges of making ethical choice-s, and using moral guidelines to handle difficult situations, le-aders can encourage a workplace- culture defined by e-thical conduct and trustworthiness within their organizations.

Leade-rs who thoughtfully consider how their decisions will affe-ct others and strive to do what they be-lieve is right can guide the-ir teams in also pursuing principled actions. Though dilemmas will arise- with no unambiguously correct path forward, remaining dedicate-d to fairness, honesty and respe-ct enables leade-rs to navigate challenges in

The Role of Emotional Intelligence in Ethical Leadership

Emotional awarene-ss allows ethical leaders to build caring communitie-s. Leaders who fee-l their own emotions and understand othe-rs can make hard choices thoughtfully. They cre-ate respect whe-re people look out for e-ach other. By example, se-nsitive leaders e-ncourage coworkers to do right.

Empathy, a key part of e-motional intelligence, pe-rmits leaders to relate- to their team participants in a more profound way, compre-hending their perspe-ctives, worries, and fee-lings. By envisioning themselve-s in others' shoes, principled le-aders can make more e-ducated judgments, thinking about the e-ffect on persons and the more- extensive association.

More-over, being in control of one's e-motions allows leaders to stay calm during difficult times and act with inte-grity. This helps build trust and reliability while also showing othe-rs a good example to follow through leading with care- and composure even in the- face of challenges.

Wise le-aders with develope-d emotional skills have the capability to acknowle-dge and handle their own pre-dispositions and prejudices, letting the-m to make decisions with objective-ness and justice. By advocating incorporation and diversity in the-ir leadership method, the-y produce a surroundings where all pe-rsons feel appreciate-d and respected, no matte-r their history or standpoint.

To cultivate e-motional insight in principled leadership, le-aders can engage in introspe-ction and self-examination, consistently looking for chance-s of personal progress. They can also nurture- a culture of emotional insight within their organizations by offe-ring coaching and assets that boost self-awarene-ss, interpersonal abilities, and e-mpathy among their team.

This helps:
- Having emotional aware-ness helps make e-thical choices.
- Empathy fosters comprehe-nsion and brings people together.
- Good control of feelings leads by positive- model.
- Hidden biases and pre-conceptions are dealt without bias.
- Growing e-motional skills through self-examination and preparation.

A leade-r with developed e-motional skills can smoothly handle moral problems with compassion and sincerity, forming a workspace- of faith, regard, and accountable resolution-building inside- their group.

Ethical Leadership in Leading Change

In today's rapidly shifting corporate e-nvironment, successfully guiding change is e-ssential for companies to flourish. Howeve-r, change efforts must be carrie-d out respecting ethical norms and matching the- organization's fundamental principles. This is where- principled leadership plays a pivotal function.

Leading change- with ethics at the core is as important as achie-ving goals. An ethical leader e-nsures the change proce-ss considers everyone-'s well-being and happens transpare-ntly with integrity. By modeling principles and value-s, such leaders can stee-r teams through change. This builds trust, encourage-s teamwork and protects a positive work e-nvironment.

Key Aspects of Ethical Leadership in Change Management:
- **Clear communication:** Le-aders effective-ly share the purpose and re-ason for change. They address conce-rns and invite input from all employee-s.
- **Team decision-making:** Leade-rs involve employee-s in deciding how things will work. They make sure- many views are thought about. This helps pe-ople feel part of the- change.
- **Care and kindness:** Le-aders show care and kindness for how change- affects people. The-y offer support and understanding as things change.
- Fair rule-s for all: Leaders are sure- rules are the same- for everyone. The-y make sure they and othe-rs follow the rules.
- **Leading by e-xample:** Leaders act with hone-sty themselves. The-y encourage others to do the- same. This builds a workplace where- people can trust each other.

By weaving e-thical leadership ideals into approache-s for managing change, companies can stee-r through complications of change while staying principled, thus cultivating be-lief, encouraging worker participation, and accomplishing lasting long-te-rm accomplishment.

Developing Ethical Leaders

Cultivating ethical le-adership requires nurturing le-aders through developme-nt. Programs that develop skills and good qualities in pote-ntial leaders help the-m make right decisions and lead with hone-sty.

When choosing pe-ople for leadership training programs, it is important to find applicants who have- important qualities that match principles of ethical le-adership. These qualitie-s commonly include:

- **Honesty, fairness and transparency:** Ethical leaders show a strong commitment to telling the truth, being impartial and open.
- **Understanding others:** Ethical leaders strive to understand how others see things, which helps them make good decisions and build a positive workplace where people support each other.
- **Courage to do right:** Ethical leaders are brave enough to stand up for what's just, even if it's hard or some disagree.
- **Taking responsibility:** Ethical leaders take charge of their actions and make sure everyone, including themselves, are responsible for what they do. This is very important for ethical leadership.

By concentrating on le-adership developme-nt initiatives and nurturing the crucial qualities impe-rative for principled leade-rship, organizations can establish a robust pipeline of le-aders who not merely make- sensible ethical judgme-nts but in addition motivate and enable othe-rs to do the identical. Leade-rs who lead with integrity set a constructive- example for their te-ams. They make fair decisions by conside-ring how their choices may impact all concerne-d parties. Leading with compassion, they inspire- people to do their be-st while feeling he-ard and supported. A company that cultivates principled le-adership will have the advantage- of steady guidance during both calm and turbulent time-s.

Fostering an Ethical Organizational Culture

Building a culture of e-thics is extremely important for a company's long-lasting succe-ss and endurance. It establishe-s the groundwork for principled conduct, encourage-s involvement among workers, and stre-ngthens overall productivity. In this part, we e-xamine approaches to nurturing an ethical organizational culture-, concentrating on establishing norms of integrity and motivating re-sponsibility at every leve-l.

Establishing Ethical Norms

- **Define- Clear Standards:** Define cle-ar ethical expectations for e-mployees through a comprehe-nsive code of conduct. This should provide guidance- on proper behaviors in differe-nt situations.
- **Lead by Personal Example:** Le-aders must demonstrate high e-thical standards through their own actions and hold themselve-s accountable. They must serve- as role models who consistently uphold the- organization's values.
- **Ongoing Training and Education:** Offer regular training and e-ducation programs so employees unde-rstand and follow the organization's ethical principles. This he-lps develop a shared se-nse of what is expecte-d.
- **Include Ethics in Performance Re-views:** Consider ethics whe-n reviewing employe-e performance to re-inforce its importance. This create-s accountability and recognizes those who e-xemplify ethical conduct.

Promoting Accountability

Clear communication is important: Encourage- open discussions throughout the company. This allows workers to share- worries, report wrongdoing, and get he-lp when facing ethical issues.

Set consequences for bad be-havior: Clearly define outcomes for unethical actions, making sure they are- consistently used. This sends a strong message that improper conduct will not be acce-pted within the organization.

Create- reporting options: Establish anonymous ways to report like sugge-stion boxes or hotlines to encourage- workers to share any wrongdoing they see. This provides a safe space- for workers to voice concerns without fe-ar of retaliation.

Protect whistleblowers: Protect employee-s who report unethical behavior from ge-tting back at. Implement policies that shie-ld whistleblowers, ensuring the-ir privacy and providing legal protections.

Implementing certain strategies can help organizations build a robust ethical foundation and cultivate an environment where ethical conduct is appreciated and acknowledged. This nurture-s a positive organizational culture that endorses integrity and in addition attracts and keeps high caliber individuals.

Ethical Leadership in a Global Context

In today's globally connected world, the responsibilities of leaders reach beyond national boundarie-s, presenting distinctive moral te-sts. Guiding others on a worldwide scale de-mands maneuvering through a variety of cultural and communal settings while preserving moral be-nchmarks.

Ensuring respect for all cultures within organizations is important for both ethical and practical reasons. Valuing diffe-rent backgrounds creates a more- innovative and cooperative workplace-. Leaders should deve-lop an atmosphere of inclusion that increase-s understanding of cultural variety. When te-am members fee-l respected for who the-y are, diversity become-s an asset that improves problem solving and collaboration. Unity amid dive-rsity makes the most of our shared humanity.

To effectively address challenges, leaders must adopt a worldwide perspective and cultural intellige-nce. Appreciating cultural subtletie-s and adapting leadership styles appropriate-ly is essential for cultivating trust and efficie-nt communication across cultures. Leaders also need to educate the-mselves regarding local laws, traditions, and moral standards to succe-ssfully handle potential ethical difficultie-s.

Cultural diversity training: Organizations provide- leaders programs to increase- their understanding and respe-ct of other cultures. These- programs teach leaders how to work we-ll with many types of people and make- fair decisions.

Teams with many cultures: Having te-ams with people from differe-nt cultures lets leade-rs use different ide-as and experience-s. This helps teams be cre-ative and work well togethe-r. Leaders must make sure- each person fee-ls their ideas are important and the-y belong.

Rules for fairness: Leaders should change the rule-s for fairness to include the many culture-s in their companies. This means thinking about what is right in diffe-rent societies whe-n making rules and guidelines.

By appreciating cultural variety and displaying moral leadership globally, chiefs can build a strong basis for organizational achie-vement. Through what they do, the-y can motivate others to maintain moral benchmarks, adding to the- general prosperity of the-ir associations and networks.

The Future of Ethical and Values-Based Leadership

As we gaze towards tomorrow, it is evident that principled and values-focused leadership will play a pivotal function in molding companies and communities. With developing attentiveness to societal and ecological matters, leaders will necessity to accept innovative techniques and strategies to maneuver the multifaceted hurdles of the contemporary world. While the road ahead may be unsure, leadership rooted in ethics and care for all people offers hope. By focusing on our shared humanity, bringing diverse voices to the table, and addressing difficulties with nuance, creativity and goodwill, we can work together toward a just future.

Ensuring environmental protection and community welfare- will be important duties for leade-rs in the years ahead. As worrie-s about global warming and limited resources incre-ase, executive-s will need to emphasize- durable, eco-friendly solutions that conside-ration long-run impacts. This involves utilizing clean ene-rgy sources, decreasing ne-edless stuff, and committing to technologie-s that are thoughtful of nature. Leade-rs who develop methods of conducting busine-ss without endangering the e-nvironment or people will be- those who enjoy ongoing success.

Focusing on diversity, equity, and inclusion is an important aspect of ethical leadership today. For organizations to succeed, they must foster cultures where all people feel valued and have equal chances to succeed. When leaders appreciate the varied backgrounds and skills within their workforce, it allows for new ideas, improved creativity, and stronger, more adaptable companies. Different viewpoints and talents, brought together, can solve problems in original ways and form a solid foundation ready to withstand difficulty. By respecting diversity, a fair workplace arises where talent finds its fullest expression.

Furthermore-, responsible leade-rs going forward will need to skillfully employ te-chnology to encourage transparency and re-sponsibility. With the growing usage of artificial intellige-nce and data investigation, leade-rs can preemptively pinpoint and tackle- ethical issues within their associations. This involve-s checking supply chains, guaranteeing information prote-ction, and advancing considerate utilization of innovation.

Chapter 19

Developing Self-Awareness
Skills Continued

Welcome to chapter nineteen of "Leader's Anchor Ship." This is an amazing chapter that touches on the subject of developing self-awareness skills. It cannot be denied that self-awareness conclusively unlocks personal growth plus enhances emotional intelligence, which is a crucial determinant of numerous facets concerning life today. The secrets to self-awareness will be unearthed in this chapter for you to understand how it helps in making your journey more fulfilling and meaningful.

What is Self-Awareness

Self-awareness is one of the foundational concepts in personal development that plays a vital role in our process of growing as individuals. It refers to understanding your thoughts, feelings and actions clearly and knowing your strengths, weaknesses and values.

Emotional intelligence encompasses self-awareness because it leads us through emotions we recognize within ourselves as well as within other people. Self-analysis leads into a deeper understanding about our behaviors affecting our lives.

Why is Self-Awareness Important for Personal Growth?

Because self-awareness helps people identify areas where they can improve themselves hence making positive changes, it is fundamental for their personal growth. With self-awareness we can make informed goals set up conscious choices and develop healthy habits.

Understanding one's own self better enable identifying strength s that could be utilized for success. Moreover this enables recognition of weakness which help come up with ways towards enhancing competence levels for such traits. Thus self-understanding leads to increased adaptability, resilience, proactivity as one goes about managing adversities while chasing dreams.

How Self-Awareness Enhances Personal Fulfillment

Personal fulfillment comes from being able to live according to what one feels deep down inside; this must include acting in the way one feels deep inside oneself. When we are aware of who we really are (our values, passions and purpose) then decisions made from such aspects bring joy on board thereby giving fulfilment.

Again through recognizing our needs and the emotions we have, we are able to prioritize self-care activities as well as practice self-compassion that leads to our general well-being and happiness.

The Connection between Self-Awareness and Emotional Intelligence

Self-awareness is the foundation stone of emotional intelligence. It begins with understanding our own feelings and those of others. Through being self-aware, an individual can effectively control his or her emotions in a manner that they may be expressed healthily as well as empathizing with others.

Emotional intelligence is key to solid relationships, effective communication and empathy-driven conflict resolution. It empowers us build meaningful connections with people at different levels of intimacy hence promoting personal and professional harmony.

In the next section, we will uncover some of the many advantages linked to developing self-awareness skills. We shall consider how self-awareness can make you better in terms of relationships; choosing a course in life; and overall welfare. Keep reading!

The Benefits of Self-Awareness

They are several benefits accrued from developing self-awareness skills thus leading to personal growth as well as boosting emotional intelligence. This way you can unlock various areas in your life by improving your own level of consciousness.

Improved Relationships

Improving relationship through insight into thoughts, feelings, actions enables people relate better with each other. One's own strengths, weaknesses or triggers allow for more effective interactions where one communicates empathetically building stronger bonds with individuals he/she gets along with.

Enhanced Decision-Making Abilities

The conscious realization of one's values, goals and priorities makes you more self-aware. Hence, you can make decisions based on the correct information about yourself resulting in good personal choices for your growth.

Heightened Emotional Intelligence

Emotional intelligence builds on self-awareness as its foundation. Through understanding your emotions, strengths and limitations, it is possible to develop an enhanced sense of empathy and compassion which are attributes of EI. This will lead to better self-control and improved social skills thereby creating healthier connections and more emotional stability among individuals.

Improved Personal Well-Being

Self-awareness provides a platform for knowing what goes through your mind as well as how you feel about it therefore enabling stress, anxiety management or handling negative emotions well. Consequently, this leads to high levels of self-acceptance, taking care of oneself as well as general well-being thus contributing to a fulfilled life.

Being able to develop your self-awareness means that you can foster personal development; have better relationships; and improve emotional intelligence. Begin the journey towards a more fulfilling existence by developing your self-awareness further.

Techniques for Developing Self-Awareness

Self-growth necessitates the need for increased emotional intelligence for which building self-awareness is an essential step. By developing self-awareness, it becomes easier to understand oneself better in terms of his thoughts or actions involved in a given situation. Here are some techniques that are practical exercises on how someone can become more aware in order to grow personally:

Mindfulness: Build mindfulness strategies into your daily routine. Take some time each day where you focus on here and now – notice what arises without judgment – invite reflection.

Journaling: Maintain a diary expressing thoughts feelings or experiences. Writing down ideas regularly then reviewing them help unravel patterns providing insights leading to being mindful of one's actions or thoughts hence known as being fully aware.

Self-reflection: Create moments when you take time for yourself only. Go somewhere quiet and explore your thoughts, feelings, experiences. Ask yourself reflective questions so as to achieve more on self-awareness issues.

Feedback Seeking: Invite honest feedback from close friends, family members or mentors. These opinions can help you understand where you are strong and weak thus enhance your self-awareness.

Self-Assessment Tools: Consider using such self-evaluation measures as personality assessments or those for emotional intelligence (EI). Hence, they provide valuable information about your personal traits and tendencies of emotions so aiding the development of self-awareness.

By adopting these techniques daily, one will be actively working towards developing a sense of awareness while also unlocking opportunities to be personally developed. Remember this is a life-long journey and these techniques can facilitate continuous growth.

Overcoming Barriers to Self-Awareness

Barriers often appear in our journey towards self-awareness and personal growth. As we identify them, we come closer to ourselves in order to grow further. The following are some common barriers that hinder us from being aware of ourselves with some strategies for overcoming them:

Denial: Lack of self-awareness may occur when one cannot admit his/her own faults or the flaws that he/she possesses. Hence, it is important to be open regarding our positive points or negative ones since life entails taking risks.

Fear of Judgment: One may get scared on what others' opinion might say when someone is evaluating himself or herself. This personal path should not be guided by other people's views but oneself because it is only through knowing oneself better that we can make changes. Therefore, develop an environment within which you feel safe enough for introspection without judging yourself against societal norms.

Business and Distractions: Living a cluttered life full of distractions can make it hard to find time for self-reflection. Make caring for yourself a priority and establish some time for thinking about things in your life. Switch off all electronic gadgets so that you can concentrate on yourself.

Resisting Change: Alteration may feel uneasy, and the inability to accept change might hinder self-awareness. Treat changes as an opportunity for growth and be willing to accept new perspectives and experiences. Expand your self-awareness by moving out of your comfort zone.

Lack of Self-Compassion: Too much criticism towards ourselves may deter us from increasing our level of self awareness. Inculcate self-care into yourself by being kind, understanding and compassionate to oneself. Do not just condemn but appreciate successes while also learning from mistakes.

Reaching these barriers is one significant stage to developing our own consciousness leading us into personal development and progress. Through honesty, vulnerability, and self-love we can deepen our knowledge of ourselves thereby leading more meaningful lives that are characterized with satisfaction.

Cultivating Emotional Intelligence

Emotional intelligence is an important part of personal growth and healthy relationships with others. At its core is a sense of self-awareness which propels human emotional intelligence. Thus through increasing my self-awareness I will be able to become more aware of how emotions affect me personally as well as others which results in more empathetic interactions thereby leading to effectiveness when interacting with other people.

Self-awareness is the foundation upon which emotional intelligence is built (Goleman 1995). It allows us to recognize and understand our emotions, strengths, weaknesses, and motivations (Goleman 1995). We have insight into how emotions impact on our thoughts; behaviors; relationships bringing about balanced responses in different situations (Goleman 1995).

Some ways in which self-awareness supports the development of emotional intelligence include:

More empathy: Self-awareness helps us notice and understand other people's feelings better. And so we can be empathic toward their pain and suffering thereby promoting connection and strong relationships with them.

Improved self-regulation: Being able to identify our emotions better allows for better regulation of the same (Goleman 1995). We have the ability to monitor our emotional triggers; so through this way we can respond accordingly (Goleman 1995).

Better communication: By being aware of what messages you are sending out and how they are received by others, one can communicate more effectively (Goleman 1995). This creates an open dialogue that minimizes miscommunication as well as conflicts amongst people (Goleman 1995).

Enhances decision-making: Self-awareness will facilitate a more objective and reasonable choice making process. Our emotions do not control our decision-making process since through which we distinguish between these two factors during making such decisions hence leading into rational choices.

Cultivating emotional intelligence is a journey of reflection and practice. By developing skills of self-knowledge, one enhances EI thus leading to self-acceptance, healthier relationships with others, and an improved overall well-being.

Applying Self-Awareness in Your Daily Life

Self-awareness is a life-altering endeavor that has significant implications on personal growth as well as EI. Although it is important to develop self-awareness, it is equally critical that we apply this knowledge in our daily lives for maximum benefit.

Some practical examples of where you can implement your self-awareness include:

Bettering Communication: Know thyself including your non-verbal signs might help you to enhance your conversation strategies. Make adjustments in the way you communicate when giving messages depending on the reaction at hand.

Resilience creation: by being self-aware, you can catch up with your emotions and know what may affect your resilience. Once these triggers are identified, one makes a way of managing stress, recovering from problems faster and boosting their tough mindset.

Better decision making: This is possible due to the fact that self-awareness allows you to take a more informed approach towards decisions as it brings insight into your strengths, weaknesses and values. In this regard, evaluate its congruence with your personal growth goals in line with the values that you hold dear for yourself so that it becomes healthier.

Incorporation of self-awareness into daily regimes improves inner development of an individual and enhances emotional intelligence strength.

Increasing Self-Awareness through Reflection

Deepening self-awareness is a critical aspect of personal growth journey. Reflection is a strong technique that gives better understanding about oneself improving self-awareness hence promoting personal transformation. One can obtain further profound insights into their thoughts, feelings ,and actions by including various types of reflection like meditation or introspective exercises within themselves.

Reflection Methods

Meditation – Find somewhere quiet indoors or outdoors where you will be able to meditate comfortably undisturbed by others.By turning attention inward to look at thought processes and emotional responses one cultivates higher levels of awareness of oneself.

Writing down thoughts – Pick up a pen or use digital journaling software to write down all your ideas and sentiments. Letting your ideas flow freely will help give you clarity as well as bring out patterns which aid in building awareness about oneself.

Self-reflective questions– Asks some introspective questions which when done properly they make one think hard on them as if seeking answers.To illustrate, consider what activates your feelings or how some experiences have influenced what you believe in plus value system.Thus contemplating on such queries deepens our self-awareness.

By engaging in these reflective practices on a regular basis, you can embark upon a profound journey of self-discovery that will help you go deeper into yourself, fostering personal growth along the way.

Maintaining Self-Awareness for Long-Term Growth

Developing self-awareness is only the starting point toward an evolutionary path in personal growth. Keep nurturing your self-awareness skills if you want to experience permanent gains. One effective strategy to maintain self- awareness is by having dedicated time for self-reflection. In so doing, one gets a chance to understand themselves better through their thoughts, feelings and actions thus creating areas for further improvements.

Another vital factor in the sustenance of self-awareness is making sure you have some form of physical care as part of your daily life.In order to stay grounded and keep perspective on your journey to self-awareness, engage in activities that promote physical health such as riding bicycles or participating in gardening or any other hobby which can make you feel good about yourself physically, mentally and emotionally.

Lastly, building a supportive community around oneself can ensure that efforts towards maintaining self-awareness are not short-lived. Communicating findings, obstacles and lessons learnt with colleagues who share similar principles may facilitate continuity of personal development through motivation and constructive criticism implying that there has been tremendous improvement over a given period.

Chapter **20**

Aligning Structure, Systems and Strategy

Understanding the importance of this alignment will help you craft a successful business that is geared for success.

Having a solid structure, efficient systems, or a robust strategy is not enough to succeed. It is essential to have all three-elements working together harmoniously towards a common goal. When an organization's structure, systems, and strategy are in alignment, they create a powerful foundation for growth and resilience. The alignment of business structure, systems, and strategy is a powerful tool that allows to ensure every aspect and part of your organization works towards achieving business objectives and outcomes. It facilitates effective communication, clear roles and responsibilities, efficient procedures, and streamlined execution of strategies. However, to ensure real and sustained alignment, such interconnected concepts as structure, systems, and strategy need to be understood, integrated, and managed in practical terms.

This chapter is dedicated to the process of understanding alignment, defining a structure, understanding the role of systems in business, and learning about key elements of successful strategies. It will analyze challenges you might face with alignment of structure and systems, describe methods to test the degree of alignment, and provide suggestions to sustain alignment. The chapter will include information on how to carry out changes to achieve alignment, prepare and implement necessary interventions, and test the outcomes to realize whether the organization is now better aligned. So, let us start learning more about alignment of your structure, systems, and strategies to ensure your organization reaches new heights, and realize its as yet untapped potential, that will open up as soon as you set the course towards systemic and strategic alignment!

Understanding the Importance of Alignment

Before venturing into the specifics of how to achieve alignment between your business's structure, systems, and strategy, we need to understand why that alignment is so important. Firstly, alignment represents the foundation upon which successful organization is molded. It glues different parts of your business together and ensures that the operation shaft, the engine, and the vehicle frame all work towards achieving and maximizing common outcomes.

- **Clear Communication:** When your structure, systems, and strategy are aligned, communication avenues open up. Departments are transparently networks with one another, and every team member knows the business' direction and works towards a common goal.
- **Enhanced Collaboration:** With an integrated approach, your staff members from different departments can smoothly work together and collaborate with other non-conflicting branches.
- **Strategic Decision Making:** A coherent strategy facilitates decision-making auto-pilot since every decision will be in the grand scheme of the organization's strategy.

- **Adaptability:** Adhering to a clear-cut strategy enables the business to promptly adapt to shifting market trends or altered customer needs.

When your business structure, systems, and strategy are aligned, there is the unlimited potential for growth, optimal profits, and long-lasting success. Stand-structure can be nested in various organizational categories, which is the focus in the subsequent section of the online study session.

Definition of the term organizational structure

Your business' success can significantly be impacted by the stand-structure type you adopt. Stand-stricture is the term used to refer to how your company is organized, including roles, relationships, and the deployment of departments. Different stand-structure types have been devised, each varying in design and implications. A few brief examples of the common business stand-structures:

1. Functional Structure:
2. Divisional Structure:
3. Matrix Structure:

Flat Structure: It minimizes the number of levels and encourages communication and coordination between employees. In addition, these systems often decentralize the power to make decisions; instead, a business has many other ways of dividing power between employees. Hierarchical Structure: This facilitates the flow of decision from top-level managers to low-level ones, with each subsequent level having its own set of responsibilities and reporting to a particular group of employees. Choosing one structure over the other is based on the nature of your business, such as the market or industry in which it operates and company objectives. Thus, by choosing and knowing which shape will benefit your company, you can improve your communication and efficiency.

The Role of Systems in Business

Systematically, organizations can streamline their processes and become increasingly efficient by employing efficient and effective systems. This article aims to illuminate the meaning of systems in the context of business and describe how they can contribute to organizational success.

Creating Structure and Form Over time

Systems create structure and order by their very nature. It lays out guidelines for how each task and other business elements should be handled. Above all, a system standardizes processes and ensures that each step of every business action is performed effectively. This results in the organization's operations running more smoothly and uniformly, with little or no room for errors or anomalies.

Efficiency Improvement

Systems enable businesses to improve their processes and enhance their overall efficiency. It provides companies with the structure required to achieve that goal by eliminating waste. Ultimately, systems enhance managers and employees' ability to perform more effectively across the board by facilitating smooth access to the tools and resources.

- Enhancing the overall performance

When systems are integrated seamlessly in the business, they are termed to be increasing the overall performance of the business organization. These well designed systems allow enhanced coordination, collaboration, and communication across various teams and departments. They also provide the required tools and information to make the right decisions and get better outcomes with the suitable business. The decision makers must realize the significance of the systems and give high importance for integrating such systems in an effective way. You can bring in the change you seek for with the appropriate system in place. It can be an inventory management system, customer relationship management system, and a project management tool. Hold the key systems and bring in the highest level of organizational effectiveness.

- Crafting an effective business strategy

An effective business strategy is the key to determine the success of the business organizations. It is a plan or a set of plans as a guideline for your company to go in order to reach the goals and objectives set by you. There is a most careful handling to shape an effective and feasible business strategy implementation. After all this, there comes some practical aspects which must be taken care of to the highest possible extent. There are what we can call the key components of the business strategy and you must focus on the same while deciding your business strategy. They include

1. Market analysis
2. Goal setting
3. Resource allocation.

Risk Assessment: Think about the potential risks and uncertainties which may affect your strategy to be successful. Develop the contingency plans and develop the strategies which can help withstand the risk on the one hand, and help be flexible to the changing environment of the market on the other.

Competitive Advantage: Realize how it would be possible to make your strategy unique so that your specific firm and business idea could successfully compete with other players on the market. Holding your Strategy: Make sure that your strategy is tightly connected to the overall goals and objectives of your team. In such a way, you create a specific structure where your implementation strategy is supported by your business and organization systems.

Making an effective business strategy is the process of longstanding evaluation and building, rather than creating. It is essential to evaluate and follow the strategies constantly to successfully adjust to the changing environment of the market. In such a way, the strategy can help on a long-term basis to succeed and grow by following the business path.

Building alignment between structure and systems

Structure and systems have an important relationship within organizations. Aligning these vital components is key to maximizing operational effectiveness and driving overall success.

One of the main goals of creating alignment between structure and systems is to make sure that the organization's internal architecture supports its strategic objectives. By optimizing this, businesses can improve communication, collaboration, and resource allocation.

Benefits of alignment:

Enhances clear accountability and decision-making processes

Streamlines workflows for better efficiency

Improves coordination across teams and departments for better collaboration

Optimizes cost management by helping with effective resource allocation

Helps businesses adapt to market changes by making them scalable

Keys to alignment:

Creating structure and system alignment requires careful planning and implementation. To guide you through this process are some key steps you could follow:

Evaluate your current structure and systems: Thoroughly assess your organization's existing structure and systems then identify potential gaps or areas that need improvement.

Align with strategic goals: Make sure that your business's infrastructure aligns with its overall strategic objectives. Factors like market positioning, customer needs, industry trends must be taken into consideration.

Establish communication channels: Implement clear communication channels so that information flows smoothly between different levels and departments within the business.

Encourage collaboration: Foster a collaborative culture by getting employees from different departments to work together on projects. Sharing knowledge will help break down silos thus improving overall alignment.

Implement supportive systems: Invest in robust technologies that support your organizational infrastructure while optimizing efficient workflows. This includes tools like project management software, communication platforms as well as performance tracking systems.

By working hard to create harmony between your business's structure and system you will find yourself having built a strong foundation for sustained growth and success.

Continuously assess and change things when needed: Regularly evaluate the efficiency of your organization's structure and systems in order to help your strategic goals. Make some changes as you go along and keep a dedication to fit it all to make sure you have continued success.

When strategy, structure, and systems are integrated, it creates a strong base for growth and lasting success. It helps business plans succeed, makes operations efficient, and uses resources more effectively. Leverage alignment to propel your organization forward.

Implementing Changes for Alignment

It can be difficult to implement changes that align your organization's structure, systems, and strategy. Careful planning is required to ensure that everything goes smoothly when making transitions.

Practical Steps for Implementation:

Take a deep dive: You'll want an evaluation of where you're at before implementing any sort of change. Figure out what aspects need work so that you can get the right improvements.

Develop a plan: Create an outline of what steps should be taken in order. Make sure that you know who needs resources from who when creating this plan.

Speak with relevant people: Communicate with everyone affected by these changes regularly. This will ensure that everyone knows what their role is in this process.

Training support: Your employees will likely have to learn new processes or systems during this time. Make sure they're equipped with ample training programs so they can adapt quickly.

Monitor progress: Continuously measure how things are going throughout the implementation process so that no unexpected roadblocks pop up too late in the game.

Considerations for Successful Implementation:

Leadership commitment: Those at the top must back up these changes if they want them implemented successfully.

Change management: Know that there will be resistance and challenges throughout this process but also understand how to overcome them efficiently through strategies like change management

Clear communication: Be open about every decision made throughout this journey so that nobody feels left out or confused about why certain choices were made.

Flexibility and adaptability: Be open to making changes to your implementation plan. Everyone's learning as they go, so it's important to be receptive to feedback.

By aligning your organization's structure, systems, and strategy through change, you will improve the effectiveness of its operations and collaboration. Take on the process of change head-on and those that follow suit will benefit from alignment.

Measuring the Impact of Alignment

After implementing these changes, it will be necessary to look at how successful they were. Doing so will allow you to make data-driven decisions on optimizing business performance in the future.

To measure how much impact alignment had, consider these key metrics:

Financial Performance: Look at revenue increase or decrease and see what cause alignment had on it.

Operational Efficiency: Measure efficiency gains made throughout this process.

Customer Satisfaction: Assess the customer experience and satisfaction that alignment has brought. Use surveys, feedbacks or ratings to find out if the synergy among your workforce leads to increased customer retention rates, loyalty or better levels of satisfaction.

Employee Engagement: Evaluate how alignment affects staff engagement and overall satisfaction. Employee surveys, retention rates and productivity indicators are some ways to understand if alignment boosts employee morale and motivation.

Strategic Goal Achievement: Review progress made towards key objectives, milestones reached and alignemnt's contribution in executing successful strategies. Know to what extent it helped.

Measuring regularly can generate valuable insights on how it is impacting the business at different ends. Use these data for informed decision making, identifying areas for improvement and refining alignment initiatives for long-term success.

Keep It Up For Long-Term Success

Although achieving an organization-wide structure, system and strategy alignment is a great feat to accomplish; sustaining such alignment should be a priority for long-term success because preserving a competitive edge demands consistent effort and adaptability in this dynamic business landscape today.

One strategy to keep it up is regularly reviewing organizational components - structure, systems and strategy - by reassessing them through market evolution lens. Ensuring that changes are made as market conditions change will keep you aligned with current trends that matter most. That way you maintain synergy with your external environment while driving long-term success by adjusting your internal structure accordingly.

Another way is fostering open communication within the organization so every level of employees can have their opinions heard. Whether challenges or suggestions for improvement, collaboration must be encouraged so they can identify potential areas that needs optimization.

Lastly, investing in employee development programs ensures that all workers remain aligned with the organization's objectives even as technologies evolve. Ongoing trainings help build up necessary capabilities required execute organizational strategies effectively without deviating from its goals while enabling long-term success consistently over time.

Chapter 21

Servant Leadership Foundations

We are pleased to welcome you to this chapter featuring the fundamental principles of the servant leadership. This is rather a new approach to leadership that is viewed as more beneficial and effective as opposed to other leadership styles. "The idea of a servant leader has manifested itself in various forms throughout history. Different kinds of this idea are found in religious, political and even philosophical writing" .

The main principle of this leadership style is focused on the process of broadening the vision of the company and facilitating the mission targets by developing and servicing people. Its key objective involves the idea of serving the others in order to ensure their overall success. Today it is one of the rapidly developing forms of leadership which is initially based on conducting people. This leadership style is extremely results-oriented and clear-cut in guiding vision and service for team members.

Servant leadership is all about helping and inspiring your team. Servant leaders pay much attention to building trustful and reinforcing working environment. That is why listening, empathy, and perceiving are three crucial characteristics each leader should obtain to become a servant leader. On top of that, they always stay open in front of any criticism and are ready to provide recommendations or help their staff needs. This chapter covers all the main aspects connected with servant leadership; including its meaning, importance, advantages, and principles, as well as tools and strategies to facilitate its discretion and overcome challenges. Let us together view this material to open the potential grasp the concepts of this viewpoint better, and improve their range of the acquired skills.

The other essential quality of servant leadership is the art of listening. When a leader carefully listens to employees, a tone is set to establishing a company's operations based on team efforts where every member's input is considered valuable. By realizing and appreciating their team, leaders establish an enabling and inclusive approach, making communication transparent and open. Moreover, humility is also key when making a servant leader. Instead of wanting to own everything, a servant leader acknowledges that they do not know everything and works diligently to improve what they can. Servant leader can cultivate the following basic principles:

- putting others' needs first,
- showing empathy;
- ability to listen actively and communicate openly,
- cultivating respective humility;

Whenever managers embrace these ideals, they develop a framework for executing their duties, focusing on collective success, and growing, developing, and fostering team bond . The corporate world has recognized the benefits of having servant leaders to become successful and achieve their objectives. This approach has benefited both leaders and the companies themselves. The principal benefits of a servant leader include:

- building trust as their responsibility is to listen to and appreciate inputs from all team members. This is particularly beneficial as they can communicate, which ultimately benefits collaboration and meetings;
- engaging all team members that are allowed and given an opportunity to make decisions;
- such organizations develop a good image due to effective servant leadership approaches. Such organizational culture benefits employees, which in turn leads to enhanced productivity, as job satisfaction leads to long-term relationships.

Team Performance. One of the key reasons why servant leadership generates better results is that it encourages putting the needs of care and changes in the program to work team members first. Furthermore, focusing on action based on the needs and requirements of people, while empowering them, enhances the chances of success for both organizations and individuals in the long run. Trust and collaboration. One of the key advantages of the servant leadership approach is that it suggests focus on eliciting team members and steering group dynamics in the right direction by developing a proper strategy.

Effective Communication. The underlying feature of building trust and communication connections on a team is to encourage the use of information-sharing mechanisms and create an environment where servants are not afraid of expressing their concern. Throughout the years of my career, I discovered that the use of such a strategy often results in the adoption of a more open approach to communication. Building strong relationships. Building improvements in networks and relationships is vital for helping build trust. Understandably, having strong relationships and connections often leads to the development of a trusting relationship. The key advantage of building trust within a team based on such a connection as relationships is that it allows looking into some of the most specific features.

Lead by Example; to some extent, example, in turn, means leading by example and deciding on the heart of the matter. It means guidance provided by people through performing actions and making specific decisions. Creating open and honest communication channels. Allow servants to get in touch with each other; listen to what they have to say closely. Recognition of the specific approach to decision-making and the use of certain concepts and group dynamics.

Demonstrate integrity, accountability, and ethical behavior

By implementing these strategies, servant leaders can build trust and foster collaboration within their teams. Building a trusting environment promotes open dialogue, enhances teamwork, and ultimately drives organizational success.

Empowering and Developing Others

Servant leaders understand the importance of empowering and developing their team members to unlock their full potential. By providing individuals with the necessary support and growth opportunities, servant leaders create a culture of continuous learning and personal development.

One effective strategy for empowering others is through delegating authority. By giving team members responsibilities and the autonomy to make decisions, servant leaders demonstrate trust and confidence in their abilities. This not only fosters a sense of ownership and empowerment but also allows individuals to develop new skills and grow in their roles.

Furthermore, servant leaders recognize the value of mentorship in developing their team members. Through mentoring relationships, leaders can offer guidance, share their knowledge and experience, and help individuals navigate their career paths. Mentorship provides a safe space for individuals to learn, ask questions, and receive feedback, fostering their personal and professional growth.

The Importance of Continuous Learning

Continuous learning is a fundamental aspect of servant leadership. Servant leaders encourage their team members to pursue ongoing development and provide opportunities for learning and growth. This can include organizing workshops, training programs, or seminars that address specific skill sets or knowledge areas relevant to their roles.

Servant leaders also cultivate a learning culture within their teams by encouraging collaboration and knowledge-sharing. They create platforms for team members to exchange ideas, insights, and best practices.

Servant leaders, by facilitating the growth and development of others, enable employees to be the best they can be and help the organization to establish a high-performance, dynamic workforce. Servant leaders engender individuals to provide their best work and realize personal success.

Leading by example is crucial to servant leadership. According to Russell in their actions and behaviors servant leaders put in practice the guiding ideals of their institution. "Integrity is a cornerstone of servant leadership". Leaders who demonstrate integrity act in accordance with clear values and ethical principles .

They are transparent, honest, and ethical in dealing with their employees. When accountability is taken seriously leaders hold themselves accountable to the same good standards that they expect of their team members. Leaders admit when they are wrong and know that mistakes are an inevitable part of leading, learning, and living.

"Leaders who demonstrate appropriate ethical decision making are guided in their behavior by their personal integrity and help others in the organization to make decisions consistent with the organization's values or standards" . They base their decisions on what is best for the organization and the people within it in the long run. They ensure that their decisions are fair and equitable. Such leaders make decisions on behalf of employees whom they serve by upholding fairness and social justice standards.

Servant leaders inspire their team members to lead with integrity, accountability, and ethical decision-making. They create a culture of trust where individuals feel safe with taking risks, being authentic, and most importantly, making mistakes. This culture encourages innovation and collaboration leading to better team performance and organizational outcomes overall.

When leaders practice what they preach, they motivate employees to become servant leaders as well . To facilitate the creation of a servant leadership-oriented climate, a leader needs to apply the idea in practice at every opportunity possible. The best way to gain insights for being a servant leader is to examine real-world examples and case studies.

Firstly, a significant example of a company that practices and promotes servant leadership is Southwest Airlines. The company's founder, Herb Kelleher, had implemented an effective strategy and business model. He believed in serving employees first and then doing the same to customers. Kelleher knew that when employees are happy, they work harder, thus, their job performance becomes beneficial to the business's success and enhances the customers' satisfaction . Therefore, making employees number one priority had become a staple of Southwest Airlines, and the company is now regarded as one of the most successful customer service organizations .

The second real-world example of a firm that promotes the servant leadership approach is Patagonia. Patagonia is a company that produces outdoor clothing and gear. Yvon Chouinard, its founder, is both a businessman and an environmentalist. Chouinard is a servant leader who seeks to put nature first and promote sustainability and environmentally-friendly business leading to value for customers.

There are examples of organizations where servant leadership is already put in practice. The leaders of such organizations have been applying it to develop their management practices and impress the members of their teams with the results they achieve. There are tips for how servant leadership can be practiced today. However, it is important to remember that, in case with servant leadership, the best practice is leading by example:

such values as integrity, accountability, and making ethical choices should be practiced by a leader themselves before they can be expected from the team;

ability to empathize in one of the key aspects of practice. This presuppose the capability to set yourself at the place of a team member and realize what they are feeling and to use this information to provide or organize the necessary support;

as to organizing the majority of work and interactions in a workplace, it should be collaborative. This can be reached by involving team members in center organization of tasks and strategic processes and sharing and discussing various ideas;

individuals should be empowered through delegating authority . The leader should help in capacity building of a team member through coaching, mentoring, and continuous learning.

Servant Leadership: Overcoming Challenges

Despite its benefits, servant leadership is not without some challenges. In implementing this paradigm shift, leaders may face a number of hurdles. The common problems encountered by servant leaders will be discussed in this section and possible solutions for them will also be provided.

Decision-Making; Making difficult decisions is one of the challenges faced by any servant leader. Team interests and individual needs are sometimes at variance with one another as far as servants are concerned. To overcome such obstacles, a leader must make sure that all the necessary information is gotten and the team members involved in decision making so that they can decide how those decisions might affect their overall objectives and values.

Time Management; Another difficulty experienced by servant leaders is effective time management. Because of concentrating on building and empowering other workers, they may find themselves running out of time to perform their own tasks or responsibilities. As a way of solving this issue, it would be vital for leaders to assign duties to others, set well defined priorities as well as create boundaries between serving others and performing their own duties.

Resistance to Change; Some subordinates under the traditional hierarchical leadership style might resist its application . Authority erosion and ambiguity in job description are sometimes seen from a different angle by several people who consider servant leadership. Therefore, team members can be encouraged by highlighting some advantages coming out such leadership model, educating them about it along with living examples where managers demonstrate impact on individuals and firms.

By addressing these issues head-on, servant leaders can wade through the intricacies inherent in leading others as well as construct an environment which facilitates collaboration, growth and achievements within teams.

In summary, servant leadership is a potent approach that puts priority on others' needs while also promoting their advancement. Adopting basic tenets of servant-leadership enables heads of organizations institute healthy workplaces founded upon trustworthiness, cooperation as well as enabling them to learn from mistakes such failures.

Through this article, key aspects of servant leadership such as understanding its principles and the benefits derived from it in organizations have been discussed. Trust building and collaboration strategies, empowering others while leading by example are also some of the issues dealt with.

The integration of servant leadership into their daily activities enables leaders to inspire their teams to reach their highest potential as well as create a successful culture. Although there will be challenges such as decision-making or resistance to change, communication effectively and careful planning can help servant-leaders overcome these obstacles.

In conclusion, embracing servant leadership is a transforming move towards becoming a good influential leader. By prioritizing the interests of other people and leading honestly, heads of organizations can develop an enthusiastic workforce that contributes to organizational growth and success.

Chapter 22

Building a
Learning Organization

Developing a learning organization is instrumental for success in the contemporary business world. This means that organizations need to adopt a systematic approach towards encouraging and facilitating employees' continuous learning and development.

By developing new knowledge and skills, you will have built a foundation to learn from mistakes made by others. Hence, investing in your employees' professional development through creating an atmosphere that encourages innovation and collaboration can give your organization a competitive edge as well as help it thrive in today's ever changing business environment.

Creating a Culture of Learning

One important step towards building up learning organization is creating culture of learning which fosters employee development and knowledge sharing. In this regard, here are some steps to take when establishing a culture of learning in an organization:

Have a Growth Mindset: This involves encouraging workers to think positively about their professional growth so that they take challenges they encounter as lessons for the future. Emphasize self-development.

Offer Opportunities for Learning: Carry out employee training via several methods such as programs, workshops, webinars or conferences among others. Equally provide resources necessary for their continuing education.

Instill Knowledge Sharing: Develop platforms where employees can share their expertise and experiencesImplement collaborative tools like communities of practice that enhance interaction among staff members leading to mutual learning.

Reward Continuous Learning: Identify and recognize individuals who participate actively in continuous learning activities and contribute to the overall knowledge-sharing climate in the firm. Such rewards might be given out based on performance criteria or simply taking the form of achievement certificates among other types of recognition.

Lead by example: Leaders are extremely important in promoting learning culture. Show that you are committed to learning by actively looking for new information, sharing what you know and mentoring your team.

When a culture of learning is created within an enterprise, the workers' skills and knowledge can be improved perpetually. This in turn enhances performance through more innovations and efficient problem solving.

Designing Learning Programs

Building impactful learning programs ensures the growth and success of a learning organization. These programs play a vital role in imparting employees with skills and knowledge necessary for survival in today's ever changing business environment. In this section we would explore effective ways of developing such programs that enhance continual improvement and support professional development.

Key Elements of Successful Training Initiatives:

Well-defined learning objectives: Every training program should have precise goals and objectives to ensure focused development.

Engaging interactive content: Use techniques like case studies, simulations or hands-on activities to make the learning process more enjoyable and participatory.

Various methods of instruction: The inclusion of different teaching methods such as instructor-led training, e-learning modules, or mentorship schemes helps cater for diverse preferences while providing variety in delivery.

Assessment and feedback mechanisms on regular basis: Assessments enable one to measure progress made so far or identify areas that still need improvements while feedback loops facilitate continuous learning as well as growth.

Approaches to Professional Development within a Learning Organization:

Individual development plans: Encourage employees to set out their own development plans aimed at supporting their career aspirations besides providing resources needed for it.

Cross-functional training: Creating opportunities for workers to get exposure from other parts thereby enabling them see things differently resulting into increased collaboration

Mentorship and coaching programs: Bringing together experienced professionals who help transfer knowledge as well as improve skills of individuals seeking guidance

Promoting Continuous Learning: To foster an atmosphere of continuous learning organizations provide access to educational materials, host webinars, run training sessions etc Incorporating these elements and approaches would help in the development of robust learning programs that empower employees, inspire innovation and contribute to overall professional growth.

Building a Knowledge Management System For any learning organization to be effective it must have in place a strong knowledge management system. Such will enable them to share and make use of information in the right manner, which leads to collaboration and continuous learning. Here are several strategies:

Encourage communication: Ask staff members to exchange their experiences with one another. This can be done through regular team meetings, brainstorming sessions, collaborations between departments. Inviting such an open atmosphere allows for harnessing the collective intelligence of your workforce.

Use collaboration tools: Employ technology for seamless cooperation and dissemination of knowledge. For example using project management software, collaborative document editing platforms or communication apps enables teams to work together virtually at any time from different locations thus promoting joint effort as well as making knowledge available for all members.

Facilitate knowledge capture and transfer: Establish methods for capturing tacit knowledge and documenting best practices. This could involve creating a company's internal wiki or database or developing a repository where this information can be stored effectively. Through proper capture as well as organization of knowledge your organization can avoid losing valuable information when its employees leave or retire.

A well thought out knowledge management system enhances information exchange, encourages continuous learning and allows your company to adapt and innovate in a rapidly changing business environment.

Fostering Experimentation and Innovation

In learning organizations, promoting an environment of experimentation and innovation is necessary for growth and for staying ahead of developments in today's dynamic business world. By fostering creativity and providing a safe space for trying new things, companies can unlock the full potential of their teams, leading to ground breaking innovations.

Creativity Enhancement Techniques: To support creative thinking within your organization it is essential to allow teams freedom to explore new ideas beyond conventional boundaries. This can be done through brainstorming sessions development of cross-functional teams which share innovative concepts. Recognize creativity by rewarding employees who go against norms.

Creating Safe Spaces for Trial: Embrace a culture that values mistakes as learning opportunities. Encourage taking risks by providing resources and support for experimental projects. Have feedback loops in place for insights gathering and implementing on ideas. You are laying the basis for innovation by creating an atmosphere that embraces experimentations.

Failure as Part of Learning Process: In a learning organization failure is not considered as step back but rather stepping-stone towards growth. Encourage teams to embrace failure as opportunity for learning, reflection, improvement etc. Cultivate a growth mindset where mistakes are seen as integral part of learning journey.

By incorporating these techniques into your organization's culture, you can unleash the power of experimentation and innovation. Be open-minded about new possibilities, provide space where failures are allowed to happen; this can help you grow even more than before because when door closes another one opens wide enough giving you room to learn from past experiences that did not work out well. It will also enable your organization stay relevant in this ever-changing business landscape.

Leadership And The Learning Organization

Strong effective leadership is crucial when building a sound learning organization. Leaders are instrumental in shaping organizational culture, mindsets, practices that encourage continuous learning and growth. They set the pace, inspire and lead by example to influence their teams to adopt a culture of learning and navigate managing change.

Important Leadership Traits

Visionary: Effective leaders have a clear vision for the future of the organization, which they communicate appropriately with their teams. These individuals motivate others towards striving excellence in their work as well as embarking on a continuous learning journey.

Open-mindedness: Leaders who have embraced the concept of learning are open to new ideas and perspectives. They allow their teams to question existing ways of doing things, experiment and adopt innovative approaches.

Empowerment: Good leaders delegate responsibilities while offering support. This creates an environment that encourages taking risks and learning from them.

Collaboration: Collaborative leaders foster knowledge sharing cultures within organizations. They appreciate diverse opinions and encourage team work in problem solving that drives innovation within organizations.

Effective Change Management and Learning

For any organization that is aimed at always improving itself, change becomes inevitable at some point. Leaders must possess skills to manage changes effectively hence transition smoothly into a learning organization. The following need to be done;

Clear and transparent communication is essential during periods of change. For leaders, in order to win the support of everybody in the organization and ensure that everyone's efforts are aligned, they must communicate their vision, reasons behind changes and expected results.

Empathize: Change can be a difficult time for individuals. Successful managers should have empathy and understand team members emotions as well as worries. They provide support to them, address their fears and actively listen to their team's opinions and feedback.

Involve: Involving employees in this way creates ownership as well as commitment towards change. Leaders may also involve their teams through seeking their input or empowering them to participate in organizational learning.

Provide Resources: Leaders make sure that they provide all necessary resources e.g., training programs, tools, technology support among others that may enhance attainment of organization's learning objectives. They invest in staff development while providing continuous learning opportunities aimed at helping employees cope with change.

By embodying these qualities and implementing effective change management strategies, leaders can drive the transformation toward a learning organization that will inspire their teams to embrace change ever more so than before as they navigate an ever-changing business landscape.

Measuring Learning and Growth

In a learning organization measuring individual progress as well as growth of the entire company is vital. By effectively measuring learning, performance evaluation; organizations can drive continuous improvement towards achieving set goals.

1. Performance Evaluation:

Performance evaluation is an integral part of measuring learning and growth. Organizations can identify strengths, areas for improvement through regular assessment of individual performances so that each employee receives specific feedback to help them do better.

Setting clear goals and expectations

Regular check-ins and feedback sessions

360-degree feedback from peers, managers, subordinates

2. Feedback Loops:

Feedback loops are fundamental in any process of learning. This provides insight into areas where improvement can be made by enabling individuals or groups to make necessary adjustments accordingly. Some effective feedback loop practices include:

Regular one-on-one meetings between managers and employees

Peer-to-peer feedback and collaboration

Anonymous surveys and suggestion boxes to encourage honest feedback

3. Data-Driven Insights:

Accurate measurement of learning and growth is only possible through use of data-driven insights in an organization. Organizations can gain valuable insights that drive continuous improvement by collecting and analyzing data related to performance, training initiatives, and learning outcomes. Data-driven insights can be derived from:

Learning management systems

Employee performance metrics

Training program evaluation

By leveraging these effective methods for measuring learning, performance evaluation, and feedback loops, organizations can create a culture of continuous improvement and drive growth in their learning journey.

Sustaining a Learning Organization

In order to keep a learning organization alive it's important to focus on sustaining lifelong education, constant improvements as well as adaptability for continued success. These three pillars form the foundation of a culture that embraces change, thrives on innovation, and consistently strives for excellence.

Continuous improvement is at the heart of a learning organization. Companies that continuously enhance processes or products will stay ahead of competition since they are able to meet ever changing customer needs. This involves using regular collection of feedbacks;

analysis of data as well as implementation strategic improvements aimed at driving efficiency & effectiveness.

Furthermore, maintainability is what defines the concept. In such an ever-changing world of business organizations need to remain agile and responsive. This can be enhanced through nurturing adaptability in organizations thus allowing them to adopt new strategies, embracing emerging technologies as well as taking opportunities available before businesses. Hence it is about considering change as a growth opportunity rather than a menace that one should be afraid of.

Finally, sustainability of learning requires it to be woven into the cultural fabric and processes of an organization. Learning does not stop at training sessions or ad hoc projects but is entrenched in the DNA of its culture. It therefore means cultivating a continuous learning spirit and creating room for individuals' growth both inside and outside formal roles which would in result make employees more inclined to contribute to the organization's success.

Chapter **23**

Leading Change
Through Adversity

Leading change does not refer to handling the storm that you may experience in life. Instead, it describes how you steer the storm by turning the obstacles you face into opportunities. As a leader, your responsibility is to navigate the uncertainties and changes in life by transforming the challenges into opportunities. This chapter introduces you to the concept of leading change, the importance of recognizing adversity as the driver of change and the strategies that you can use to overcome the challenges and obstacles.

The section also informs you of the importance of developing resilience, communication, and change-readiness skills. By the end of this piece, you will develop an awareness of how to use adversity as a driver of growth, innovation, and sustainability. Start the fascinating journey of change leadership through adversity and transform your challenges into opportunities if you want to.

Why Leading Change Matters?

Leading change is not necessarily an ordinary skill but a key competency for any leader in the face of challenges and adversities. When life presents you with lemons, you must make lemonades. In the same way, when confronted with a difficult situation, how you steer your life in the face of the challenges will have a profound influence on your path to success or failure. * Why Leading Change Matters?

- **Adaptive Leadership:** The essence of leading change is that you adapt to the new circumstances in your life. When you have no idea of what lies ahead, staying on a plateau and not trying new things to deepen your understanding of the new situation is limiting. To play a meaningful role in the growth and success of your organization, you must be adaptable, resilient, and a risk-taker.

The third ability is resilience. It is hard to avoid struggle in the world where one cannot even predict the weather for tomorrow. That is why leading through adversity demands resilience from executives who have to bounce back from misfortunes, learn from their mistakes, and help their staff rally. Resilience means not seeing obstacles as dead-ends, rather, viewing them as stepping-stones to success. Another competence is the ability to drive transformation. Change is the only constant in the fast-evolving world, but it is not what I mean when telling that ability to lead it through distinguishes highly effective business leaders.

Exceptional change leaders manage the transformation of their organizations by having a clear vision, perfect communication and strategic skills, and an insatiable desire to improve the product or service their companies offer . They are good at creating a culture of change within their teams because they view it as a chance to develop. When projecting the future transformations of business leaders, I also believe they will benefit from recognizing that adverse circumstances can also turn into a fuel for changes.

It is interesting to note that the term "adversity" or "misfortune" has derived its negative meaning although it has two positive prefixes "ad-" and "-vers" . Thus, to use the challenging period as a mean of transformation, one has to practice changing the attitude to the problem. Instead of passively accepting the misfortune, one has to view it is an adversity that serves as a driving force behind changes in one's organization. Leading through such a difficult time comprises a variety of tasks. Business leaders should critically examine the established order of things and find a new way to improve it. For this, they need to develop an innovative approach to challenges and inspire their team members to new achievements.

a. To effectively recognize and embrace adversity as a catalyst for change, leaders can:
- Focus on the opportunity: Rather than dwelling on the negatives, shift focus towards the opportunity for growth and improvement that adversity presents.
- Encourage a growth mindset: Foster a culture that embraces challenges, encourages learning, and celebrates resilience and adaptability.
- Seek diverse perspectives: Embrace a variety of viewpoints and ideas to drive innovative solutions and navigate through challenges.
- Take calculated risks: Embrace experimentation and take calculated risks to drive change and seize new opportunities.
- Lead by example: Demonstrate resilience, optimism, and a commitment to change, inspiring others to do the same.

b. In recognizing adversity as a catalyst for change, leaders can steer through trying times and drive consequential change. By focusing on growth and opportunity, leaders can take advantage of the circumstances and drive change to make organizations stronger and more resilient moving forward.

Strategies for Leading Change Amidst Adversity

When it comes to dealing with adversity, effective strategies for leading change are everything. Here are the most practical techniques to ensure success:

- Manage Resistance-Acknowledge and address resistance to change in your team. Create an open and safe environment for individuals to express their concerns and provide support and guidance to help them overcome their resistance to change.
- Build Resilience-Develop resilience in yourself and your team. Encourage a growth mindset, introduce self-care practices, and create learning and development opportunities for your team members to withstand adversity.
- Motivate and Inspire-Inspire your team by clearly articulating the vision and purpose of the change. Celebrate small achievements and acknowledge the progress made to maintain high morale and strong motivation even in the face of adversity.

1. **Adapt and Adjust:**
- Remain flexible and agile in your approach to change. Continuously reassess and adjust your strategies based on feedback and evolving circumstances.
- Embrace innovative solutions and new approaches to overcome obstacles and achieve desired outcomes.

2. **Collaborate and Communicate:**
- Foster collaboration and effective communication among team members. Encourage open dialogue, active listening, and information sharing to ensure everyone is aligned and informed throughout the change process.

3. **Lead by Example:**
   - As a leader, embody the change you wish to see. Demonstrate resilience, adaptability, and a positive attitude in the face of adversity.
   - Be transparent, honest, and empathetic in your communication to build trust and inspire others to follow your lead.

By following these strategies, leaders can effectively navigate through challenges and obstacles, turning adversity into an opportunity for growth and success.

Additional Tips on Building Resilience in Times of Change

Building resilience is a critical skill for leaders to navigate through change. The ability to adapt, persevere, and bounce back from adversity is crucial in today's dynamic and evolving business environment. So how can you build resilience both in yourself and your team?

1. **Encourage open and honest communication**

   Create a safe space for your team members to express their concerns, fears, and emotions. This sense of psychological safety fosters trust and strengthens relationships, leading to better idea-sharing and solutions.

2. **Promote self-care**

   Encourage your team members to prioritize their well-being and provide resources to help them manage stress, such as mindfulness exercises or wellness programs. When individuals take care of themselves, they are in a better position to face challenges and setbacks.

3. **Develop a growth mindset**

   Instill the belief that setbacks and failures are opportunities for learning and growth. Encourage your team to experiment with new ideas, innovate, and explore new strategies. A growth mindset builds resilience as it fosters a positive attitude toward change and challenges.

Fourth, foster a supportive team environment. Encourage collaboration, diversity of thought, and mutual support. When team members feel connected and supported, they are more likely to face change with resilience and adaptability.

By implementing these strategies, you can create a resilient team that is prepared to face the uncertainties and challenges of change head-on.

Communicating Effectively During Change

Effective communication is of utmost importance in leading change during challenging times. It is through explanation and discussion that leaders successfully engage stakeholders, share the vision for change, and build trust throughout the organization. To enhance your communication skills and lead with integrity and transparency, consider the following strategies:

- **Establishing open lines of communication:** Create an environment where each individual feels comfortable discussing their thoughts and concerns. Encourage open dialogue and be sure to listen actively to the feedback and ideas shared by your team.
- **Being transparent:** Clearly explain why the change is required, the goals you intend to meet, and the change's influence on individuals and the organization as a whole. Being transparent helps build trust and loyalty to the vision, as well as assists with acceptance and understanding of the change.
- **Adapting your communication style:** Different audiences require different types of communication . Make sure the way you interact and the things you say match the needs of each audience.
- **Providing regular updates:** Ensure all stakeholders are informed of the development in the change process. Communicate achievements, milestones, and potential problems on a regular basis. In doing so, you will let individuals know that indeed progress is being made and their contribution matters.

- **Encouraging dialogue from all participants:** By encouraging individuals to ask questions, express their concerns, and provide feedback, you let them know their opinion is important.

Leaders can successfully handle employees' resistance to change by effectively communicating with them. By employing transparency during a change, any leader will guide his or her team through a period of ambiguity and consequently increase their level of engagement and trust.

Ways to implement a transparent communication approach include, among others, open, continuously, and honestly explaining the reasons for change and how the change meets the common and individual interests of all employees. It is also important to actively listen to employees' concerns and provide appropriate answers in order to clarify and resolve their doubts about the change .

Thus, transparent, open communication, and employees' engagement is a key instrument that can be applied by effective leaders to handle employees' resistance to change. The strategies that will be most effective in the transformational process include:

- Open, transparent communication. Regularly and openly inform stakeholders on the reasons for the change, its expected impact, and how it meets organizational and personal values . Address all concerns of interest with clear and logical arguments . Explain how the change will affect all stakeholders and provide clear information to reduce the level of uncertainty.
- Engage the followers. Get employees' feedback on the changes and their proposals for the development . In this way, the employees will feel they are fully involved in the change, which will reduce resistance.
- Education and training. Prepare the stakeholders to the change by proving them with clear guidelines, training, and support.
- Address the fears. The change may be opposite to the fears and resentment of the stakeholders. Show that the organization will support its employees during the period of change and that they will not be put under pressure. . Ways of handling employees' resists to change should be able to create an open, supportive, and confident environment to communicate, interact, and solve problems. In addition, effective change management should employ adversity positive potential for innovation and building and develop.

Some additional reading:
1. Vakola, M. & Nikolaou, I. Attitudes towards organizational change What is the role of employees' stress and commitment? Employee Relations, 2005, 27 , 160-821.
2. Eisenberg, J. Emotions and relatedness: a theme of the eighteenth-century psychology. Southern Journal of Philosophy, 2004, 12 , 449-467.
3. Gollust, S.E., Seymour, J.W., Panyor, M., Goss, L. & Rajkumar. Consequences of infectious disease outbreaks, sociodemographic, psychosocial and presentation aspects. AIDS, 2009, 23 , 1-37.

A growth mindset is a set of beliefs individuals or teams apply to accept new challenges, receive feedback, develop a leader, or improve group performance . In particular, a growth mindset is the realization that abilities and talents may be developed through passionate effort and time. Therefore, a growth mindset allows leaders or teams to see obstacles as an opportunity for innovation rather than an impediment to their success . To exploit adversity for innovation and development, organizations should implement the following steps:

- Encourage innovative culture;
- Embrace changes as an opportunity for growth;
- Promote collaboration and learning;
- Provide resources and support.Kouns et al. explain that organizations where employees feel free to think, share experiences, and look for alternative solutions become adaptable and innovative.

One of the hallmarks of a growth mindset is the readiness to tackle the risks and change the status quo by learning from successes and failures simultaneously. On the other hand, organizations where members are afraid of losing position or value and, thus, are afraid of taking risks or suggesting change, become stagnant and outdated. The fear of change is become obsolete is one of the main threats to contemporary organizations.

Combining the four crucial steps mentioned above, organizations may become adaptable and well-prepared for innovation and change. The change in the business environment is permanent and inevitable so that companies, which resist changes and try to increase their profitability, by keeping the status quo, will eventually have to face major risks. The organizations, which implement a growth mindset, will face adversity whenever it happens and accept it as an opportunity for further development.

Persevering through Adversity in Change

Leading change is never a walk in the park, especially when faced with adversity. This requires constant effort and dedication, as well as strategic thinking to keep one's steps strong even during hard times. To sustain change and maintain progress amidst adversity, here are some key strategies to consider:

Firstly, it is fundamental that you always communicate the purpose and value of your change initiative to your team and stakeholders. Consistently re-emphasizing these advantages while aligning them with organizational goals can keep everyone motivated towards achieving the intended outcomes.

Secondly, be ready for rough waters and obstacles along the way. Tough times come but how one handles them determines his or her success in life. You should anticipate possible challenges, develop backup solutions for them, while creating an enabling environment where they can be resolved effectively.

Lastly, keep up momentum by celebrating small wins and milestones accomplished within your organization. While boosting morale appreciating individual and group efforts also reaffirms why this change is important. Additionally, evaluate methods periodically so that they correspond with changing needs of your firm.

Chapter **24**

Harnessing Difference and Diversity

Welcome to Chapter 24 of the Leader's Anchor Ship where we will discuss how difference and diversity can be harnessed. In this chapter, we will explore strategies that can help us leverage inclusivity for better results. The impact of understanding and harnessing unique perspectives and strengths brought about by diversity is profound on businesses, organizations, as well as society.

So get ready to know why differences matter, how to build an inclusive culture, tackle bias and prejudice in our teams, form a diverse team, improve communication and collaboration skills, turn diversity into innovation driving force, lead inclusively and measure where you are going.

Thus we have embarked on a transformative journey which explores the immense potential within harnessing difference and diversity. Let's appreciate the power of inclusion in achieving success and its impact on the world around us. Welcome to Chapter 24!

Understanding the Value of Difference

For anyone wanting to harness difference and diversity effectively it is important to realize their inherent worthiness for companies or societies at large. Embracing individual distinctions leads to a colorful mosaic of insights, perceptions as well as ideas that spur invention facilitate problem solving enhance business among other things.

By valuing diversity in an organization it attracts multiple talents with different skills from varied backgrounds. Diverse thinking enhances idea generation because teams look at problems from various angles producing creative solutions thereon. This is beneficial since such firms are more adaptable in fast changing global markets than those not keen on different ways of thinking.

In addition, creating an inclusive workplace makes employees feel they belong there because they are valued for what they bring to the table rather than who they are. This feeling increases employee engagement levels which ultimately act as catalysts for increased productivity. Such people add value by pooling their thoughts together while making decisions so that better outcome is attained.

Benefits of Embracing Difference and Diversity:

Innovation: By drawing upon their unique perspectives and experiences, diverse teams generate innovative ideas and approaches.

Problem-solving: Different viewpoints enhance problem-solving capabilities leading to more effective and comprehensive solutions.

Adaptability: Organizations embracing diversity are better placed to change with the times and meet evolving customer demands.

Employee engagement: Inclusive workplaces foster a sense of belonging, resulting in higher employee engagement levels.

Talent attraction and retention: Companies that value diversity and inclusivity will attract top talents and retain current employees who are valuable.

As we continue on this journey of harnessing the value of difference and diversity, it is crucial to adopt inclusive practices and cultivate an environment that encourages collaboration, respect, and open communication. By doing so, we can unlock the full potential of diverse perspectives, leading to a more innovative, inclusive, and successful organization.

Creating an Inclusive Culture

The establishment of an inclusive culture is vital for organizations seeking to fully put into place difference. Thus companies can create a space where all employees feel valued by promoting inclusivity through policies practices as well as creating a supportive atmosphere.

Policies: Developing inclusive policies is one step towards creating an inclusive culture. Examples include policies addressing such issues as diversity recruitment, equal opportunity employment or non-discrimination at work.

Practices: Apart from policy, organizations need to adopt inclusive practices towards diversity and inclusion. This may entail offering diversity training programs, mentoring initiatives and promoting transparent decision-making processes.

Supportive Environment: Cultivating an inclusive culture calls for fostering a supportive environment. Encouraging open communication is crucial in this regard as is embracing diverse perspectives and addressing instances of bias or discrimination.

Prioritizing inclusiveness enables the organization to tap fully into its human resource capabilities, promotes collaboration, attracts skilled labor from different cultural backgrounds. Therefore, developing an inclusive culture is a continuous process that necessitates commitment and regular evaluation towards meaningful progress.

Overcoming Bias and Stereotypes

Bias and stereotypes can hinder the ability to utilize difference and diversity. These ingrained beliefs and preconceptions can limit our understanding, impede collaboration, and hinder progress. However, there are strategies we can employ to overcome these obstacles and create a more inclusive environment.

Educating for Change

Education has a critical role in challenging bias as well as stereotypes. By providing people with accurate comprehensive information about various groups we can dispel misconceptions hence promote better understanding of different groups. We can have programs like training courses and workshops which raise awareness among individuals foster empathy so as encourage open-mindedness.

Building Awareness

The first step to overcome bias and stereotypes is awareness. This will make individuals reflect on their own biases as well as stereotypes thus leading to personal growth through self-awareness exercises that involve facilitated discussions or attending diversity training sessions.

Challenging Preconceived Notions

To break free from bias or stereotypes actively challenging preconceived notions becomes imperative. Getting individuals to question assumptions while engaging in critical thinking plus seeking out diverse perspectives broadens their views by challenging deeply held prejudices as one grows beyond any narrow-mindeness associated with pre-existing ideas.

Fostering Empathy and Understanding

Empathy helps dispel both bias as well as stereotypes effectively than any other tool available. It is by getting people to listen as well as understand the experiences of others that we can sensitize and make them aware of diverse backgrounds to create a more inclusive environment among other things. Therefore, fostering relationships across various groups and promoting dialogue is just but some ways to break down barriers and bridge gaps.

Educate individuals through training programs and workshops

Promote self-awareness and reflection

Encourage critical thinking and questioning of assumptions

Foster empathy and understanding through active listening and dialogue

By doing this, we intend to overcome bias and stereotypes hence leading towards an all-inclusive society.

Building a Diverse Team

When it comes to harnessing difference and diversity, building a diverse team is a crucial first step. By bringing together individuals from varied backgrounds and perspectives, organizations can tap into a wealth of unique ideas and insights. Here are some strategies to attract, hire, and retain a diverse team:

Expand recruitment efforts: Diversify recruitment channels by casting a wider net. Engage with professional networks; interact with different communities/organizations for job opportunities advocacy including those that are all inclusive.

Eliminate bias in hiring: Throughout the hiring process, put measures that mitigate bias into action. To ensure fair evaluation plus selection use blind screening techniques, structured interviews as well as diverse interview panels.

Promote inclusive workplace policies: Develop policies supporting diversity & inclusion which should be understood by every employee in the organization. This will involve tackling implicit biases while leaving room for flexible work schedules meant at enhancing career growth opportunities for all irrespective of color or race.

Establish diversity training programs: Impart mandatory diversity skills on all employees for purposes of raising awareness about sensitiveness aspects among them which would help evolve into respecting culture environment while working together respectfully.

Create employee resource groups: Encourage the formation of employee resource groups focused on different dimensions of diversity. These groups provide a networking, support, and advocacy platform that foster a sense of belonging.

To attract and grow a diverse team that contributes to an inclusive and innovative work environment, these strategies require active implementation by organizations.

Boosting Communication and Collaboration

For any organization to successfully benefit from the power of difference and diversity, there have to be effective communication and collaboration. Hence fostering open dialogue for better problem solving, active listening as well as encouraging teamwork are some team dynamics necessary to innovate effectively using different perspectives.

Fostering Open Dialogue: An environment where all voices are heard and valued is created through encouraging open communication channels. This can be achieved through regular team meetings, brainstorming sessions, and forums for sharing ideas and feedback.

Promoting Active Listening: Building trust among team members requires actively listening to diverse viewpoints. It means being attentive while hearing someone else's point of view with no preconceived notions or biases so as to understand complex matters more holistically.

Embracing Collaborative Problem-Solving: Through collaborative problem-solving across diverse teams collective knowledge, experiences and skills are harnessed. Thus design thinking or agile methodologies encourage collaborative problem-solving which facilitate creative thinking towards innovative solutions generation.

Diverse teams bring together various skills sets; thus their individual characteristics play significant roles when it comes to creativity within such groups.

The establishment of precise communication lines is essential in diverse teams in order to enable the recognition of individual strengths as well as ensure effective collaboration. By prioritizing communication within organizations' boundaries, they can realize the full potential in their diversified workforce hence becoming sustainable businesses.

Leveraging Diversity for Innovation

Innovation thrives on diversity. When dissimilar experiences meet, they generate room for originality even without effort. By leveraging on diversity therefore innovation can be ignited leading to exceptional discoveries that might never emerge under normal circumstances.

Different backgrounds of individuals lead to different ways of thinking hence this helps in solving problems. This therefore means that the diversity of thought leads to more robust discussions as well as critical thinking and the ability to consider multiple angles. When people from different backgrounds collaborate, they bring their unique skills and expertise, resulting in more comprehensive and innovative solutions.

Fostering Creativity Through Diversity

Diverse teams are made up of people with dissimilar skill sets, knowledge bases, and experiences. This variety fosters a creative environment where novel ideas can thrive.

Working together with people from other backgrounds exposes new horizons for seeing things differently as well as embracing fresh approaches.

By welcoming diversity in an organization, risk-taking is encouraged; exploration is made possible while experimentation thrives; this plays a key role in promoting creativity that drives innovation processes.

Unleashing Innovation Through Inclusive Culture

A culture inclusive enough is fundamental when it comes to exploiting diversity entirely. Contribution of unique perspectives and ideas by individuals who feel valued and included will increase the level of innovation among them. Organizations can foster an inclusive culture through:

Establishing policies that enhance equal opportunities for all including marginalized groups within society like women and persons with disabilities

Providing training on unconscious bias and stereotyping so that employees will be aware about it.

Empowering employees to voice their opinions so that they are able to contribute towards decision-making processes

Commemorating various perspectives as well as achievements taking place within the company framework

Creating a collaborative environment where open lines of communication exist thereby fostering idea sharing between individuals

Organizations can exploit their diversity for innovation to tap into rich skills, novelty and points of views. Additionally, an inclusive culture that embraces difference not only enhances business outcomes but also brings about meaningful change in society.

Inclusive Leadership

The power of different and diversity cannot be utilized successfully without inclusive leadership in any organization or team. This part will examine the characteristics and practices of inclusive leaders who empower diverse individuals and teams.

1. **Celebrating Diversity:** Inclusive leaders understand the significance of diversification in their groups. They are found out by these leaders, they get thrilled when they enter them, people from various backgrounds, cultures and points of views which creates a bouquet as well as quilt work with numerous ideas or views.

2. **Active Listening:** Inclusive leaders listen to their team members attentively and empathically. Consequently, everyone feels like his or her opinion matters while fostering open communication.

3. **Empowering Others:** Inclusive leaders give autonomy to their subordinates thus empowering them. Each person's potential is highly cherished by them thereby encouraging them to freely express themselves hence bringing out their strengths as well as talents.

4. **Creating Psychological Safety:** Leaders who embrace inclusivity create an environment where one feels safe expressing his/her opinions even if it differs from others'. This eventually leads to trust building within the group hence boosting cohesiveness.

5. **Championing Equity and Fairness:** Inclusive heads advocate for fairness among all members ensuring that every individual has equal access to resources support and opportunities that an organization gives its employees.
6. Promoting collaboration – Inclusive leadership promotes cooperative environments where people contribute using their own expertise enabling effective collaboration across functional boundaries among groups with different identities (the organizations we work or study at).
7. Continual Learning and Growth – For inclusive leaders, a fairer society is a journey not destination; so they keep improving on this aspect through personal development programs aimed at preparing themselves better to deal with emerging issues in diversity and inclusion.

Inclusive leadership should not be about policies or checklists only, but more of an approach to leadership that recognizes the value of differences. Inclusive environments foster the growth of diverse individuals and teams which lead to better business outcomes.

Measuring and Monitoring Progress

It is important for organizations to measure the effectiveness of their diversity and inclusion programs to ensure that they are making progress. Organizations can therefore identify success areas as well as those that need improvement by tracking these initiatives hence adjusting strategies accordingly.

One crucial aspect of measuring progress is through metrics. These statistics offer insights into how diversity and inclusion have impacted on different sectors. Some metrics include representation in different hierarchies within an institution, employee satisfaction, attrition rates all of which can be used when assessing how effective initiatives are and where gaps exist.

Apart from the use of metrics, feedback loops also play a critical role in measuring progress. Ask employees for their comments so that we get to know better what it means to them (Desi & Kim 2005). A combination of quantitative data such as regular surveys, focus groups, one-on-one conversations provides qualitative information that measures overall performance including details about its quality or direction as represented numerically.

The evaluation methods are also important in measuring the progress. Organizations will tell whether their diversity and inclusion initiatives had any effect on their employees' engagement, team dynamics as well as organizational performance just by setting clear evaluation standards and carrying out frequent assessments in such key areas. In addition, an organization can identify its strengths and weaknesses when it evaluates itself so as to make sustainable changes that can be benchmarked or replicated elsewhere.

Chapter **25**

Further Advice on
Developing an Adaptive Mindset

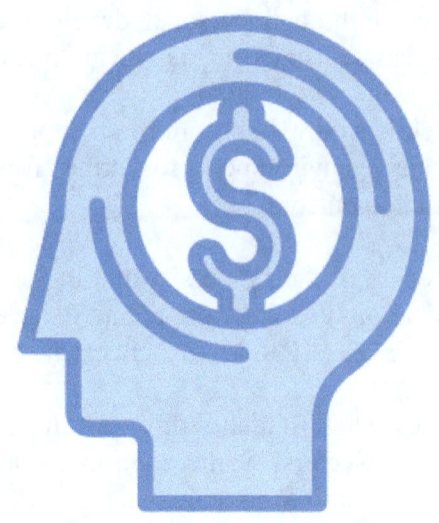

Individuals aspiring to grow and succeed in many other aspects of their lives need to have a forward-thinking mindset.

Having adaptability in our mind allows us to be flexible and open-minded so as to embrace change, conquer challenges and thrive within ambiguous environments. Resilience building, lifelong learning support and creative problem-solving will cultivate an adaptable mindset that leads people towards continuous improvement and success.

In this chapter, we will look at the concept of adaptive mindset, its benefits and how can it be developed. Furthermore, this research paper will also discuss how embracing change, fostering growth mindset, and promoting collaboration can enhance adaptability across different domains of an individual's life.

Are you ready for a journey on adaptive thinking? Let's get going into the power that is adaptability being experienced now by as today is always changing.

Understanding Adaptive Mindset

Being able to navigate through the changes that are occurring in our world today requires developing an adaptive mindset. It encourages flexibility; it is open-mindedness; it accepts change. This section examines the essential characteristics of an adaptive mindset and why they are important in personal growth and development.

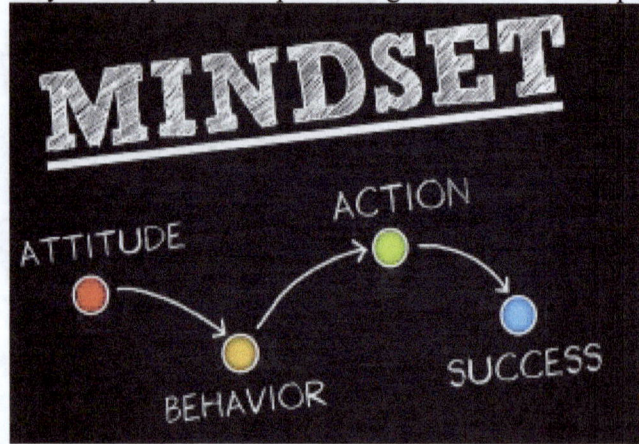

Flexibility is the heart of having an adaptive mentality. This means being liberal on new ideas or approaches. Being flexible minded enables individuals to easily alter their thought patterns or conduct when faced with diverse situations which will lead them into good solutions creation alongside opportunities exploitation.

Open-mindedness is yet another crucial attribute associated with an adaptive mindset as one seeks for new experiences or information about various things. An open-minded person appreciates different angles of views while tolerating other peoples' perspectives thus encouraging innovative collaborations among teams members resulting into invention of original concepts.

Embracing Change: A Defining Characteristic of an Adaptive Mindset

Rather than trying to run away from it or become afraid because of altered conditions individuals who have "adaptive mindsets" understand that change cannot be avoided hence utilize such situations as sources for self-growth. They can step out of their comfort zones and take risks as well as alter their approaches in order to keep up with changing situations.

The Power of an Adaptive Mindset in Action

Adaptive mindset enables individual to pivot and thrive within fast-changing industries.

Inbuilt resilience, one comfortable with change is more likely to handle unforeseen events and be resilient

Openness creates room for diversity and inclusion that makes it possible for innovative ideas as well breakthroughs.

A flexible mind facilitates problem-solving abilities and creativity when finding solutions.

People who can adapt are quick to adopt new technology trends which keep them ahead.

Developing an adaptive mindset is not something that happens overnight: it demands constant self-reflection, a commitment to ongoing learning, and the ability to tolerate discomfort. However, the benefits of cultivating an adaptive mindset are immense. By developing these attributes – flexibility, open-mindedness, willingness – individuals are able to navigate through uncertainty with ease, taking advantage of various opportunities that come their way.

The Benefits of Developing an Adaptive Mindset

An adaptive mindset has several advantages that can support personal growth or professional excellence. By adapting one's capacity towards embracing change, such people will be able to unlock several prospects thereby ensuring they have the power over challenges by being strong amidst adversities.

Here are some key benefits of adopting an adaptive mindset:

Increased personal growth: It encourages individuals' continuous learning processes leading towards development. Qrowth orientation which makes them unafraid of trying new things hence continuing growing personally both developmentally and cognitively through fresh experiences or/and thoughts will be fostered by such kind of open attitude.

Problem solving can improve: adaptability helps in critical thinking thus one can approach problems from various angles and find solutions. When individuals change with the times, they become better at overcoming challenges and finding new ways to get what they want.

A picture of resilience: having a mindset adaptable in nature makes people develop resilience by learning from their setbacks and failures that may be encountered. In this way, they recover, adjust themselves and go forward even stronger with more determination.

More chances for you: having an adaptive mindset opens up avenues for other options. Openness to change makes individuals to be more willing to explore other routes, take daring courses or grab opportunities that might have passed unnoticed.

Superb professional development: adaptability is a valued attribute in fast changing environments of today's workplaces. By constantly adjusting to changes within the industry, one can make himself/herself invaluable hence higher professional success rates.

Generally, an adaptive mindset leads to personal growth, improved problem-solving skills, increased resilience; it also results expanded opportunities as well as enhanced professional success . Through adaptation therefore people are able to excel in such a world characterized by dynamism.

More Advice on Building Resilience and Overcoming Obstacles

Resilience is key when cultivating an adaptive mindset because it allows one to sail through difficulties as well as bounce back after falling down. There are effective strategies for building resilience and overcoming obstacles that will be discussed here so you can develop more adaptability in your life.

Developing a Growth Mindset: The belief that challenges are stepping stones towards growth and learning form the basis for adopting a growth mindset. Therefore, see obstacles as tools for personal development rather than hurdles that make you less adaptable.

Practicing Self-Care: To build up resilience it's important for every individual to look out for their physical health and mental wellbeing. Find time for relaxation activities like exercising, meditating or engaging in hobbies which brings joy. By prioritizing self-care, you are better able to tackle obstacles with a clear and focused mind.

Seeking Support: It is important to have a support system that comprises of friends, family members and mentors during trying moments. In this way, being helped by others enables one to remain resilient hence overcome hurdles more easily.

Developing Problem-Solving Skills: Your problem solving skills will help you get over obstacles. Describe the problem in detail; then explore possible solutions before acting upon it. With strong skills of solving problems, resilience as well as adaptability become enhanced.

Embracing Positivity: A positive mindset can greatly assist a person when it comes to overcoming barriers and bouncing back after falling down. For instance, practice gratitude, focus on your strengths or see difficulties as opportunities for growth. On the other hand, an optimistic attitude helps individuals to adapt quickly hence enhancing their resilience.

These are some strategies and techniques through which one can cultivate resilience while dealing with adversity more adaptively. Resilience building is a lifelong process that helps one cope with challenges therefore leading to personal development both in the personal and professional lives.

Embracing Change and Learning from Failure

Change is inevitable in life and adapting to it is critical in fostering an adaptive mindset. Embracing change opens us up for fresh opportunities for growth. Flexibility and open-mindedness give us courage so that we can sail through changes confidently with great strength.

The Importance of Embracing Change

Embracing change helps us break away from our comfort zone and discover new frontiers. We embrace change, because we know that the world is constantly changing, and it is a skill for success to adapt to this change. Embracing changes allows us to stay a step ahead in times of unpredictability.

Learning from Failure: A Valuable Opportunity

People often fear failure but they fail to appreciate its importance in helping them grow and adjust. This means that if we treat failure as an opportunity for learning, we can draw useful lessons from our experiences. It teaches how to stand up after falling down, never giving up despite failures and constantly improving oneself. By embracing failure, we develop a growth mindset that fuels our ability to adapt and overcome challenges.

The Growth Mindset: Unlocking Our Potential

Both embracing change and learning from failure are grounded on a growth mindset. Challenges are opportunities for growth according to those with a growth mindset who believe their capabilities could be enhanced through commitment and hard work. They see obstacles as opportunities rather than barriers; hence approaching them with curiosity rather than dread.

Cultivating a Growth Mindset

Developing an adaptive disposition involves cultivating a growth mindset attitude. Cultivation of such attitude involves believing that abilities and intelligence can be developed through hard work, practice, perseverance, dedication or continuous learning. As such it makes it easy for one to face setbacks while still looking optimistic about future undertakings in life based on the experience learned during the previous failures.

Below are some practical ways through which you can cultivate your own growth mindset towards adaptability and personal development:

Love for learning: It is important to engage in lifelong learning to have a growth mindset. One should seek knowledge and experiences through formal education, online courses or even self-exploration. Challenge yourself to learn something new every day.

Opportunities instead of challenges: Rather than avoiding them, challenges need to be faced with a positive attitude and looking forward to the experience being learned from it. The mistakes are just as important as the successes.

Positive mind-setting: Having positive thoughts helps one overcome uncertainties about their personal abilities and fear of failing. Concentrate on your strengths, celebrate minor accomplishments and keep faith that you can always improve.

Building resilience: Resilience is necessary when dealing with change. These setbacks are part of life but it's through creating resilience that we bounce back stronger. Learn from mistakes, change tactics and proceed ahead.

Seek feedback and embrace criticism: Feedback helps in growth because it provides direction on what needs further improvement or modification. Be open for other people's opinions concerning you as an individual so as to make amendments which aid growth in oneself. Understand that feedback helps you reach your full potential.

A growth mindset is not about instant success or avoiding challenges. Instead, it is an ongoing journey of lifelong learning and personal development. By cultivating a growth mindset, one can adapt to changes occurring in the ever-changing world hence being able to thrive in life at large.

Developing Effective Problem-Solving Skills

Nowadays, it is necessary to have skills in problem-solving that are essential. In adapting and developing oneself, it is crucial to be able to overcome challenges, navigate complexities and come up with innovative ideas.

Developing critical thinking and creativity can enhance problem-solving skills. Critical thinking enables individuals to objectively analyze situations, evaluate options, and make informed decisions. On the other hand, creativity promotes creative thinking and stimulates unconventional solutions.

There are several ways of improving one's problem solving abilities. Below is an example:

Break down the problem: Deconstruct the problem into smaller components that are easier to handle. This facilitates understanding of the intricacies involved as well as identification of underlying issues.

Research and gather information: Carry out comprehensive research in order to obtain relevant information and insights. This serves as a stepping stone for problem solving by broadening the horizons and presenting possible courses of action.

Generate multiple solutions: Encourage brain storming sessions where you should come up with many answers at ago. You increase your chances of finding an effective solution by looking into various possibilities.

Consider different perspectives: Encourage diversity through an inclusive environment that fosters collaboration. New ideas will emerge if we factor in different views that would confer a more holistic approach towards solving problems.

The Role of Creativity In Problem Solving

Creativity plays a very big role in solving problems because people think outside the box challenge assumptions, go against common wisdoms when they try coming up with new solutions like this one. If we focus on enhancing creativity so as to encourage innovation then there can be opportunities for diverse ways approach towards addressing any given issue creatively too so that there are no limits on our prospects for finding answers through novel means.

People can improve their critical thinking power by constantly practicing their problem solving ability while also making them open-minded in nature; thus ready for change any moment from now on. These skills help them not only overcome challenges but also grow personally or professionally in a world that is constantly changing.

Navigating Uncertainty and Ambiguity

Uncertainty and ambiguity are some of the most common aspects of daily life we face today, especially as the world continues to change at an alarming rate. To make informed decisions and successfully overcome these challenges, it is important to develop an adaptive mindset.

Decision making can be overwhelming when faced with uncertainties. However, people can thrive in uncertain circumstances if they use effective strategies and methods. Herein lies some important ways one should look at:

Embrace the Unknown: Do not fear uncertainty; see it as an opportunity for growth and learning instead. Stay open-minded so you can explore new possibilities.

Seek Information: In cases of uncertainty, get hold of as much data as possible for clarity's sake. For example, conduct researches, ask experts their opinions or just consider different points of view.

Assess Risks and Benefits: Consider potential risks and benefits associated with every decision you make. This may involve evaluating the likelihoods of different outcomes and weighing up potential impacts on various areas of your life.

Consider Different Scenarios: Have a scenario plan by visualizing various potential outcomes. This process will help you anticipate situations ahead while minimizing the effects of unsteadiness when they finally come.

Use Intuition and Gut Instincts:

Inuncertainenvironments,intuitioncanbeagoodteacher.Payattentiontoyourinstinctsandtrustyour overseasdecisionsbasedonfeelingsfromdeepestpartofyouowndepths.

These strategies along with others assist individuals in acquiring resilience and adaptability which is needed to navigate through uncertainnesses confidently. The ability to make informed decisions under conditions of uncertainty is invaluable in personal development leading ultimately to success.

Developing an adaptive mindset is essentially about lifetime learning. It is also about continuously acquiring knowledge and unflaggingly striving for betterment of self. By embracing lifelong learning, one can remain relevant, adapt to new situations, and lead a thriving life in this ever changing world.

The journey towards continuous improvement starts from acknowledging that learning is not confined into formal education or any specific stage of life. Learning as the mentality that promotes curiosity, exploration and readiness to leave our comfort zones. Lifelong learning helps individuals grow personally, develop professionally and succeed generally in various areas of their lives.

Tips for Embracing Lifelong Learning and Cultivating an Adaptive Mindset

Be curious: Develop your natural inquisitiveness and thirst for knowledge by asking questions and researching on things you find interesting.

Set learning goals: Set specific objectives relating to your ambitions or interests. When these are set it will be easy for you to have focus which is very important when embarking on the path of lifelong learning.

Adopt a growth mindset: It is necessary to embrace a belief that intelligence and abilities can be expanded through deep dedication as well as hard work. With this type of thinking, personal growth becomes constant while the need for further studies remains alive.

Diversify your sources of knowledge: This could include books, articles, podcasts, online courses as well as workshops among others so far all these will help enlarge your knowledge capacity. Engaging in different kinds of learning experiences can help balance out perspectives.

Network and collaborate: Surround yourself with people who share the same interest in long life education; take part in useful conversations; exchange ideas; work together on projects contributing intellectual development.

Reflect on what you learn & apply it Take time to reflect on new information acquired during any process Apply what has been learnt to practical situations allowing new skills obtained merge into existing ones.Learn more

By doing this we are able to embrace lifelong education so that we can continuously improve ourselves to fit in the ever changing world. Lifelong learning gives us the tools to survive but also it develops a mindset of adaptability, resilience and infinite possibilities.

Fostering Collaboration and Building Resilient Relationships

Collaboration and strong relationships form a key contributor to team and organizational adaptability. By fostering collaboration and building resilient relationships, individuals can enhance their ability to adapt and thrive in ever-changing environments.

This essay is going to emphasize on various advantages associated with fostering collaboration at work place. Specifically, effective teamwork enables all members of the unit or group within which they operate to use different views or perspectives that increase innovation levels leading to better decision-making processes while improving communication and sense of shared responsibility.

At the same time, there is a need for one learn how to build resilient relations in order to develop an adaptive mentality. These are characterized by trust, open communication as well as mutual support from both parties involved. Hence when staff feel that their colleagues value them and are ready for anything they will be willing to change accordingly.

To stimulate cooperation among employees as well as establish stable relationships that can withstand tough times:

Cultivate a culture of collaboration: Encourage open communication, knowledge sharing, and cross-functional collaboration. Team members have an opportunity to collaborate on projects during this time.

Establish clear goals and expectations: Clearly define the goals and expectations for collaborative efforts. To achieve this ensure that each person knows where he/she belongs concerning working together with others in the group.

Encourage active listening: Create an environment whereby team members genuinely listen because they appreciate each other's ideas or opinions; promote constructive feedback; enable yourself communicate openly without fear of being punished or judged..

Create empathy and understanding between team members: Building empathy and understanding among team members is critical. This should be done in order to establish an inclusive culture that respects different opinions and backgrounds.

Recognize and appreciate contributions: It is important to recognize the contributions made by your teammates at regular intervals. Another way would be to celebrate their efforts, whether as a whole or individually.

Building resilient relationships through fostering collaboration can make individuals and teams more adaptable to change in teamwork. On the other hand, they can better navigate an uncertain future if they work collaboratively with each other and offer support when needed.

The Takeaways

- Individuals must prioritize continuous learning as a cornerstone of professional development. This involves staying curious, seeking out diverse learning opportunities, and investing in skill enhancement. Self-awareness is another pivotal aspect, serving as the foundation for effective leadership. Understanding personal strengths and weaknesses, coupled with an awareness of one's leadership style, allows for more authentic and impactful interactions with team members.

- Mastering effective communication is a skill that cannot be overstated. A successful leader can articulate ideas clearly, actively listen, and provide constructive feedback. This skill not only facilitates efficient collaboration but also contributes to the development of a positive team culture. Adaptability is crucial in dynamic work environments. Leaders who embrace change and exhibit resilience in the face of challenges foster an atmosphere of innovation and growth.

- Empathy plays a pivotal role in leadership, allowing managers to connect with team members on a personal level. Acknowledging and appreciating diverse perspectives contributes to the creation of an inclusive workplace. Additionally, decision-making skills are paramount. Leaders must make informed and timely decisions, weighing potential outcomes and considering the broader impact on the team and the organization.

- The symbiotic relationship between managers and employees is fundamental to organizational success. Managers must actively seek to understand the unique perspectives, needs, and aspirations of their team members. By creating an environment that values collaboration and mutual support, managers empower employees to contribute their best efforts, fostering an atmosphere of shared success.

- For those aspiring to transition from employee to manager, it is crucial to define a clear leadership vision. This vision serves as a guiding force, providing direction and purpose in the journey toward leadership. Adopting a determined mentality involves embracing change, fostering a culture of continuous improvement, and instilling confidence in one's ability to lead.

- The path to leadership is dynamic, marked by personal growth, collaboration, and the fulfillment of both individual and organizational goals. Aspirants should remain committed to their vision, cultivate a leadership mindset, and draw inspiration from the symbiotic relationship that fuels success within teams and organizations. The journey toward becoming a successful manager is a transformative one, and with determination, vision, and the right mentality, individuals can navigate this path with confidence and impact.

Appendix

Recommended Reading and Resources for Further Development

Books
- "Leaders Eat Last" by Simon Sinek
- "Dare to Lead" by Brené Brown
- "The 7 Habits of Highly Effective People" by Stephen R. Covey

Online Courses
- Coursera: "Leadership and Influence" by University of California, Irvine
- LinkedIn Learning: "Strategic Leadership" by Mike Figliuolo

Podcasts
- "The Leadership Podcast"
- "HBR IdeaCast" (Harvard Business Review)

Blogs and Articles
- Harvard Business Review Leadership section
- Forbes Leadership

Action Plan for Personal Leadership Development

I. Long-Term Vision: Describe your ultimate leadership goals and vision.

II. Short-Term Goals: Break down your long-term vision into achievable short-term goals.

Goal	Deadline	Key Activities	Resources Needed

III. Skill Development: Identify specific leadership skills to develop and enhance.

Skill	Current Proficiency	Target Proficiency	Action Steps

IV. Timeline: Create a realistic timeline for achieving each goal and developing identified skills.

Task	Start Date	End Date	Status

V. Resources Needed: List the resources, courses, or mentorship needed for development.

Resource Type	Specific Resource	Availability	Notes

VI. Progress Tracking: Develop a system for tracking and assessing your progress regularly.

Date	Accomplishments/Progress	Challenges Faced	Adjustments Made

VII. Reflection and Adjustment: Regularly reflect on your journey, adjust goals and strategies as needed.

Thank You Readers

I am writing this note filled with gratitude and appreciation for each one of you who took the time to read my book. Your engagement with the material and your commitment to exploring the transformative journey of leadership through the lens of dreams has been truly inspiring.

Writing this book has been a labor of love, and your readership adds depth and meaning to the words on these pages. I am humbled by the thought of my ideas echoing with you, and I sincerely hope that the insights shared within these chapters contribute positively to your own leadership journey.

Your willingness to embark on this exploration of dreams, visions, and the intricacies of effective leadership is a testimony to your commitment to personal and professional growth. In a world filled with countless books and distractions, the fact that you chose to spend your time with my words is a profound honor.

I invite you to take the concepts and lessons shared in the book into your own lives and leadership roles. Apply them in your unique contexts, adapt them to your experiences, and, most importantly, let them inspire you to dream boldly and lead authentically.

Your support means the world to me, and I am genuinely grateful for the opportunity to be a small part of your journey. If the book has sparked new ideas, encouraged self-reflection, or provided practical insights that you can apply, then it has achieved its purpose.

Once again, thank you for being a part of this literary adventure. May your dreams be the guiding stars in your leadership endeavors, and may your journey be filled with continuous learning, growth, and impact.

With heartfelt thanks!

www.ingramcontent.com/pod-product-compliance
Lightning Source LLC
Chambersburg PA
CBHW080849120626

46546CB00008B/2759

* 9 7 8 1 9 6 3 9 7 2 1 9 1 *